MW00332029

When Music Goes to School

When Music Goes to School

Perspectives on Learning and Teaching

Danette Littleton

Published in partnership with the
National Association for Music Education (NAfME)

ROWMAN & LITTLEFIELD
Lanham • Boulder • New York • London

Published in partnership with the National Association for Music Education (NAfME)
Published by Rowman & Littlefield
A wholly owned subsidiary of The Rowman & Littlefield Publishing Group, Inc.
4501 Forbes Boulevard, Suite 200, Lanham, Maryland 20706
www.rowman.com

Unit A, Whitacre Mews, 26-34 Stannary Street, London SE11 4AB

Copyright © 2015 by Danette Littleton

Poem in chapter 2 by Laura Krauss Melmed, illustrated by Ed Young *The First Song Ever Sung*, New York: Lothrop, Lee & Shepard Books, 1993. Used with permission.
Lyrics in chapter 4 "Singing in the Shower" from *Blue Moo*, New York: Workman Publishing Company, 2007 © Sandra Boynton. All Rights Reserved. Used by permission.

All rights reserved. No part of this book may be reproduced in any form or by any electronic or mechanical means, including information storage and retrieval systems, without written permission from the publisher, except by a reviewer who may quote passages in a review.

British Library Cataloguing in Publication Information Available

Library of Congress Cataloging-in-Publication Data

Littleton, Danette, 1942- author.
When music goes to school : perspectives on learning and teaching / Danette Littleton.
pages cm
Includes bibliographical references and index.
ISBN 978-1-4758-1334-0 (cloth : alk. paper) -- ISBN 978-1-4758-1335-7 (pbk. : alk. paper) -- ISBN 978-1-4758-1336-4 (electronic)
1. School music--Instruction and study. I. Title.
MT1.L69 2015
780.71--dc23
2015019874

♾ ™ The paper used in this publication meets the minimum requirements of American National Standard for Information Sciences Permanence of Paper for Printed Library Materials, ANSI/NISO Z39.48-1992.

Printed in the United States of America

To my beloved grandchildren, Gabriela, Nikolas, and Oliver

To all the children who informed my teaching
by their wisdom and goodness

To the memory of Pat Duffy Hutcheon, my mentor and dearest friend

To Rhoda Shalom for her guidance

To my mother, LaVerne Martin Littleton,
for her abiding love and faithfulness

Contents

Acknowledgments

For this successful publication, I wish to thank
Rowman & Littlefield:
Thomas F. Koerner, Vice President and Publisher of Education Books
Carlie Wall, Associate Editor, Acquisitions
Meaghan White, Associate Editor, Production
National Association for Music Education:
Ella Wilcox, Manager, Editorial Communications
David Litchfield, Illustrator, book cover image

Prologue

A Child's Mind Is a Terrible Thing to Standardize

When Congress passed No Child Left Behind (NCLB), signed by President George W. Bush on January 8, 2001, the new law mandated advantageous funding incentives that induced a narrow concept of educational reform. Public education continued the shift toward substantial standardization in curriculum and assessment and teacher accountability that had its origins in *A Nation at Risk: The Imperative for Educational Reform* (1983), a document sanctioned and distributed by the U.S. Department of Education.

At work here is a dichotomy between two philosophies of education: (1) whether student learning is best achieved by scripted curriculum, teacher-directed instruction, and standardized testing; or (2) whether student learning is best achieved by means of a child-centered, inquiry-based, content-driven curriculum. Simply asked: "What are the skills children should know and exhibit? versus "What are children's developmental capacities for learning?" Decisions on how best to teach, support, and guide children rests on the answers to one or the other of these opposing questions.

When the pendulum of educational change swings too far between these poles of thought, children and their teachers experience something resembling whiplash. However, since NCLB's implementation, the "conceptual pendulum" has stalled like a twelve-year clock. With the mechanism controlled by politicians and billionaires, the rest of us are running up and down like blind mice.

What's wrong with public education? It depends on whom you ask. George H. W. Bush said he wanted to be the education president—a reformer for better schools. His was a popular position among politicians during the 1980s and 1990s as evidenced by a plethora of "education" governors: James Hunt, North Carolina; Bill Clinton, Arkansas; Lamar Alexander, Tennessee; Richard Riley, South Carolina; George W. Bush, Texas. George W. Bush was governor of Texas from 1995 to 2000. He initiated testing policies that expanded under Jeb Bush, Florida. Some of the governors expanded funding for prekindergarten and/or raised teachers' salaries; however, most of their reforms mandated new requirements that called for student testing linked with teacher accountability and curriculum uniformity.

In February 2009 the American Recovery and Restoration Act author-
ized Race to the Top, and Secretary of Education Arne Duncan announced a $4.35 billion allocation for reward incentives to states that
compete and win the race "to create common college- and career-ready
standards and assessments." In June of that year, the Common Core State
Standards (CCSS) were initiated: Forty-eight states signed on and made a
commitment to develop teaching methods and content according to
Common Core Standards. By 2013/2014, states were expected to have
completed full implementation of the standards into their curricula; and
in 2014/2015 participating states would be prepared to administer the
new assessments.

Secretary Duncan made enthusiastic predictions for success even
while Common Core Standards were under construction and revision
and before the corresponding assessments were designed. In a speech
before the American Society of Newspaper Editors in June 2013, Duncan
spoke of the benefits of Common Core: Teachers in different states could
use the same lesson plans; a child in Mississippi would face the same
expectations as a child in Massachusetts; and children of military personnel could move across the world "without a hitch" in their schooling. He
added, "I believe the Common Core State Standards may prove to be the
single greatest thing to happen to public education in America since
Brown v. Board of Education."

Funding designated for public schools has now been made available
to private charter schools. This, from a *New York Times* article about
vouchers: "Currently, 17 states offer 33 programs that allow parents to
use taxpayer money to send their children to private schools. According
to the American Federation for Children, a nonprofit advocate for school
vouchers and tax-credit scholarship programs, individuals or corporations receive tax reductions if they donate to state-run scholarship
funds."[1]

At the same time public school funds are being siphoned off, public
schools are closing in Chicago, Detroit, Philadelphia, New York City, and
in smaller cities across the United States. According to politicians, these
school closings were necessitated by budget cuts. Data contributed by
advocates for standardization and high-stakes testing supported closing
"underachieving" schools. Unfortunately, superintendents and princi-
pals willingly complied while parents protested because their children
were transferred to other schools.

Private money that bankrolled the charter school "choice" movement
has placed public education further at risk. Big businesses have big ideas
about *their* futures, but is the corporate model good for the future of
education? Children and their achievements are not products, just as so-
called "failing" schools cannot be compared to obsolete production mills
or manufacturing plants. Children are not assets or consumer goods, nor
competitors in the global economy; and teachers are not their production

managers solely responsible for company losses. In what other *profession* would one spend an entire career in a position vulnerable to ever-changing demands where one has no place at the adult table?

Meritocracy, a model for teacher assessment, suggests that competition for advancement improves teacher accountability and performance. On the contrary, most teachers disdain ranking and salary competition with their colleagues; instead they seek collaboration and support of each other. Recently, high school teachers in Lee, Massachusetts, received merit pay funded by the Gates Foundation for their students' high scores on standardized tests. Yet the teachers rejected the payments, saying that the pay was not fair (equal pay for equal work, experience, and education); that one teacher's efforts did not result in students' test scores, rather, that many teachers had contributed to the students' success; and that the merit-based process created divisiveness among the staff. Instead, the merited teachers requested that the monies be spent on instructional supplies and materials to benefit all students.

What do teachers want? In a recent survey by the publisher Scholastic and the Bill & Melinda Gates Foundation, *Primary Sources: America's Teachers on Teaching in an Era of Change* (www.scholastic.com/primarysources/download-the-full-report.htm), 82 percent of the respondents reported that "constantly changing demands," including changes in policies, curriculum, and leadership place undue strain on their already limited time and resources. Ninety-nine percent of teacher respondents said that they have students with social, emotional, or behavioral challenges; 23 percent report having seven different student populations in one classroom, those with special needs—those who are two or more grades below grade level, and those who are gifted. While 69 percent of teachers say that they have a voice at the school level, very few are heard at the district, state, or national levels. Overwhelmingly, they express needs for more time, resources, and high-quality instructional materials for their teaching and their students' learning.

Teachers are entitled to professional wages for their work, talent, expertise, and dedication; however, it is well known that American teachers have been denied the respect and compensation afforded other professionals in law, medicine, business, the sciences, technology, and engineering. The last time teachers enjoyed unconditional respect in the United States was when young English clergymen taught future young clergymen at Harvard in 1636.

What are the effects of the testing-equals-proficiency brand of education on children, their parents, teachers, and schooling? Young children, in their prime for creating, imagining, and learning, are frustrated and dispirited by rigid, test-driven schooling. Making bubbles in kindergarten today means filling in little circles on test papers, not chasing bubbles at play. During the early years, skills-based, directed instruction has replaced child-directed activities, including opportunities to play, socialize, and freely explore learning through play centers.

Children worry that if they fail or do poorly, their teachers will be upset. Parents panic when their children do not do well on standardized tests and thus transmit their anxieties to the children. Teachers experience the stressful tension between mandated standardized testing and their commitment to a rich, varied, and developmentally appropriate curriculum.[2] The Association for Childhood Education International (ACEI) recently stated that "standardized testing in the early years causes stress, does not provide useful information, leads to harmful tracking and labeling of children, causes teaching to the test, and fails to set conditions for cooperative learning and problem-solving."[3]

Across the nation, teachers and parents are protesting standardized testing over multiple forms of assessing student learning. One preschool teacher in Chicago said that her four-year-olds are frequently being tested for "readiness." Kindergarten children in her district took fourteen different standardized tests in one year. "I find it demoralizing. Testing young children is developmentally inappropriate. This is damaging to teaching and to learning."[4]

Kathleen Oropeza, in an article titled "More Testing Madness in Florida Schools" in the August 31, 2014, *Tampa Tribune*, wrote: "Who in their right mind would subject kindergartners to seven or more high-stakes end-of-course exams? The Florida Legislature—that's who." She explains that in 2011, senators and representative passed state statute 1008.22(6) requiring school districts to administer thousands of new tests for every "course not currently addressed by state exams." This means even kindergarten children will sit for standardized tests similar to those administered to older students that may include, language arts, mathematics, music, physical education, science, and social studies.

According to the *Miami Herald*, September 2, 2014, "Out of the 180-day academic year, Miami-Dade County schools will administer standardized tests on every day but eight." Broward County superintendent Robert Runcie said that "the abundance of new tests—up to 1,500 could be introduced" in Broward school districts in 2014. So far, the new tests are not available for most of the subjects.

In addition to standardized tests, Palm Beach County will give about four hundred end-of-course exams for every student, in every subject, K–12. The new tests are needed to meet the demands of the teacher merit-pay law (the first legislation signed by Governor Rick Scott) that tied teachers' evaluations to student test scores. PBC superintendent Wayne Gent said, "It appears the primary purpose is more about teacher evaluation than what's in the best interest of students."

Jeb Bush, who served as governor of Florida (1999–2007), in the shadow of his brother George W. Bush introduced most of the educational "reform" policies that have become nationalized, that is, corporate-influenced spending to support standardized, testing-based, accountability, vouchers, charter schools, and value-added measurement (VAM) of teachers.

In a recent interview with the *Miami Herald*, Jeb Bush said critics and those who oppose Common Core testing standards cared too much about kids' self-esteem. "Let me tell you something. In Asia today, they don't care about children's self-esteem. They care about math, whether they can read—in English—whether they understand why science is important, whether they have the grit and determination to be successful. . . . You tell me which society is going to be the winner in this 21st-century: The one that worries about how they feel, or the one that worries about making sure the next generation has the capacity to eat everybody's lunch?"

We care about children's self-esteem.
We care about children's emotional, social, and cognitive development.
We, who teach, parent, and think about children
care about their well-being.

Somebody needs to tell Jeb Bush that you cannot have feeling (emotion) without knowing it; conversely, you cannot know (experience) devoid of feeling. Ergo, children's emotional state, concept of self, and understanding of others are intrinsic to their lived experience, undivided by biology and physical and cultural environments. In the same way, learning cannot be divided into cognitive skills, conceptual understanding, and affective sensitivity and behaviors. Heed the words of Alfred North Whitehead, "You may not divide the seamless coat of learning."

Over time and across cultures, beliefs about children have shifted with the turbulent winds of societal and political change. Parenting and schooling practices have predictably followed the prevailing currents. For centuries after St. Augustine's treatise on humankind, infants were judged guilty of original sin. When the concept of tabula rasa was applied to children, it meant they were blank slates; later, children were considered as empty vessels to be filled. More recently, conceptualization focused on the natural child, the hurried child, and the cognitive child. What do these labels tell us about the true nature of children? Like the tale of the blind men and the elephant, each viewpoint is derived from a singular perspective. Each one is incomplete.

Long before children enter a classroom, their hearts, minds, and brains are fueled by the need to know, explore, wonder, and play. Regrettably, at many schools today, students encounter an environment of standardization, conformity, and excessive testing that hinder rather than foster learning. Children's natural behavior traits of curiosity, creativity, and compassion wither in an arid classroom climate along with their enthusiasm and joy of learning. Disregard for the true nature of children and how they learn and develop subverts the very purpose of education. A child's mind is a terrible thing to standardize.[5]

NOTES

1. Fernanda Santos and Motoko Rich, *With Vouchers, States Shift Aid for Schools to Families*, 03/27/2013.

2. For music teachers, individualizing curriculum has become especially daunting given the demands to demonstrate and document their work according to the National Common Core Music Standards. When teacher accountability, evaluations, and retention depend on satisfactory implementation of the new standards, music teachers and music education in public schools are in peril.

3. Anna Weinstein, *Kindergarten Testing: The Realities and Dangers*, http://www.education.com/magazine/article/testing-kindergarten-realities-dangers/.

4. Virginia Meyers, "Disappearing Act," *in American Teacher*, March/April, 2013.

5. "Sometimes the most brilliant and intelligent minds do not shine in standardized tests because they do not have standardized minds."—Diane Ravitch, Twitter@dianeravitch.

Introduction

Toward Individualism, Imagination, and Inventiveness

Each teacher has a story to tell. Not only a story about teaching, but recollections of learning from childhood onward. Our shared stories are powerful exemplars of experiences as learners, each singular and one of a kind. Important to the present work is the concept of *one*, according to the individual specialties and potential of each child. As their teachers, we are mindful that the children we teach are seekers and beholders in a self-directed *curriculum of one*. Children are natural learners, innately imaginative, and predisposed toward playful people, experiences, and environments. By nature and disposition, they resist conformity, testing, and standardization; however, as children enter kindergarten today, they encounter schooling practices incompatible with their ways of learning.

Individualism, imagination, and invention, once highly valued in learning and teaching, are jeopardized by the chaos of educational reform. Those who presently teach and learn, those who parent, and many others (professors and researchers) contend that a strong storm front of standardization is pushing against child-centered learning by mandated runaway all-consuming testing—results of which are used to rank children, rate their schools, and calculate their teachers' effectiveness, retention, and pay. Even more grievous, the present testing culture opposes the culture of childhood and proves detrimental to the child's developing mind and spirit. Critical policy issues and schooling decisions are vested in how we answer fundamental questions about learners and learning: What is a child like? What should a child know?

In the present era of nationalized state-by-state standardization, regard for "what a child is like" is sacrificed for "what a child should know." This false dichotomy is patently manufactured by ill-conceived ideas of educational reform: testing improves learning, standardized curriculum raises standards, testing data exposes inadequate teachers, and all students will reach grade-level proficiency by 2014.

Less obvious, except to teachers, is the narrowing of the curriculum. We know that testing takes time away from content and instruction; and that students soon learn that if it's not tested, it's not important.

In contrast, this means that curriculum design and instructional strategies must be matched to the child's development—biological, social, cognitive, emotional, and educational—rather than the other way around whereby the child is subsumed by limited curriculum and instruction practices. While there are predictable courses of development, each child is unique, as determined by his and her genetic properties and environmental influences. In a democratic society, public schools ought to provide children nothing less than a full body of essential knowledge together with the skills of access to that knowledge. Not only will children grow and thrive, so will our democracy. Thomas Jefferson said: "I think by far the most important bill in our whole code is that for the diffusion of knowledge among the people. No other sure foundation can be devised for the preservation of freedom, and happiness."

Against a dark backdrop of a testing-based curriculum, the stage is now set for new rules affecting teaching and learning across all subjects and disciplines, including music. Some have asked, "Why should music educators be concerned about standardization since music is not a tested subject?" Simply, because the children we teach *are* being tested. It's not subject matter that is of first concern; it's children. If this seems to be a distinction without a difference, consider both of these affirmations, "I teach music to children" versus "I teach children music." Emphasis matters.

Children who are anxious and stressed by the pressures of testing and those who are discouraged by their scores are the *same children* who come to our music room. Those who have become subjugated to multiple-choice thinking, short-answer narration, and formulaic writing practices are the same children we teach. Agents of uniformity exert powerful influence on children's attitudes toward learning and their expectations of classroom life. I am concerned that, at heart, children will begin to accept regulated learning and lose their spontaneity, creativity, and self-confidence.

In response to confounding efforts to standardize (sanitize and privatize) teaching and learning, this book reaffirms that children need music. In ways that no other discipline emulates, music learning contributes to children's comprehensive development: social, *knowing self and others*, emotional, *feeling and expression*, and intellectual, *thinking artistically, creating, and inventing.*

This work upholds the purpose and significance of music in the education of children; it concurrently supports teachers' autonomy throughout the process of teaching from planning to performance. Validated and sustained throughout this book is the immense importance of teachers' dedication to originality in curriculum design, creative music instruction, and compassion for children.

What you read here is personal and decidedly iconoclastic. I do not seek to offer competing philosophies, methodologies, or a series of what-to-do-when lesson plans. I propose a model that unifies music curriculum, music repertoire, instructional strategies, and classroom procedures with corresponding theory and supportive scholarship. My goal is to invite teachers and those who wish to become teachers to participate and interact with the ideas presented here, as to engage in conversation.

This model invites you to study what you find here about why children need music, how they learn, and what methods and resources are suitable for the children you teach. It suggests that you identify what you most want to know, systematically observe children in different settings, document their musical interests, responses, behaviors, and search the relevant literature for answers. Studying, researching, observing, documenting, and applying your findings is a continuous process that increases knowledge, understanding, and skills. Teaching is an art form that demands introspection. It is by reflecting on our experiences as learners and teachers that we gain self-knowledge and see our way forward.

What follows is a series of connected, yet stand-alone, essays. Each one chronicles music learning and teaching through the voices of children and teachers and vignettes from differing and authentic classroom settings together with references from theorists and intellectuals in psychology, sociology, and the arts. As you explore these works, I hope you will be inspired, informed, and challenged by new thoughts and insights about learning and teaching.

The first chapter, *Individualism: A Curriculum of One*, establishes a perspective vital to this work. Throughout the life span, one's own perceptions, emotions, and thoughts are singular, even though our development follows predictable courses from infancy, childhood, adolescence, adulthood, and elder years. In a personal narrative of music learning and teaching, this essay suggests that we are shaped by early experiences that propel us as learners and, ultimately, as teachers. From childhood throughout the life span, learning is personal, individual, and selective, that is to say, a continuous life curriculum of one.

Chapter 2 demonstrates why play is important in children's lives and their musical development. *Imagination: The Musical Culture of Children's Play* shows how the play spirit infuses and enlivens learning and teaching. An antidote to standardization, playfulness restores joy, excitement, and creativity in the classroom. By observing children at play, teachers gain new insights into children's music making: How they play with music on their own or with others, make up spontaneous songs, improvise dance moves, create music with rhythmic and melodic instruments, and invent music stories with props, costumes, and toys.

The third chapter, *Originality: The Voices of Children*, establishes the significance of autodidactic, untaught learning, through childhood recollections of notable scientists, musicians, and writers with connection to the factors and opportunities that cultivate unconstrained learning. The function of untaught learning in the lives of children and its value to teachers in better understanding the developing child is demonstrated. At some risk, I reveal deeply personal accounts of my experiences with children, of their goodness, sensitivity, resilience when facing difficulty, and their willingness to forgive my mistakes. Embedded within the content of these narratives are discourses on philosophy of teaching and learning, ecological influences on learning, and race and culture.

Chapter 4, *Inventiveness: Making Meaningful Music with Children*, concentrates on the development of children's musical skills, and enhances their perceptions, musical understanding, and delight in music. Teachers are encouraged to customize curriculum and instruction accordingly: To rely on their own knowledge and love of music, strengthen their teaching skills, develop curriculum and instructional plans appropriate for the children they teach, and reject scripted lessons created by others.

Chapter 5, *Perspectives: Voices of Teachers*, cites viewpoints concerning the state of the teaching profession, teacher evaluation and competency, professional learning and classroom applications of the new National Core Arts Standards for Music. At this writing, the standards are being field-tested and made ready for implementation. Outlines and details for understanding and using the standards are presented on the website www.nationalartsstandards.org. The purposes are described as follows: "National Core Arts Standards are designed to guide the delivery of arts education in the classroom with new ways of thinking, learning, and creating. The standards also inform policy-makers about implementation of arts programs for the traditional and emerging models and structures of education."

Epilogue: *On the Cusp of Possibility*. Ultimately, it is my hope that this work contributes to curriculum decisions and instructional choices, inspires creativity, and encourages individuality. Moreover, I commend to you the children—all those who look to you for acceptance beyond instruction, playfulness over efficiency, and for open-mindedness to see the world with a child's-eye view. *The greatest [teacher] is the one who does not lose his child's heart.* When children's minds and hearts are young, they are eager to know and learn. They are joyful, compassionate, honest and trusting, and resilient. Their needs, to play, pretend, and explore, and to sing, dance, and make music, must be safeguarded. As their teachers, we are challenged to create pedagogy and possibilities that guarantee each child a meaningful education in music with enduring compassion and undeniable respect.

Unless someone like you cares a whole awful lot,
Nothing is going to get better —
It's not.
—Dr. Seuss, *The Lorax*

ONE

Individualism

A Curriculum of One

In a personal narrative of music learning and teaching, this chapter suggests that we are shaped by early experiences that propel us as learners and, ultimately, as teachers. From childhood throughout the life span, learning is personal, individual, and selective, that is to say, a continuous life curriculum of one.

From childhood, some of my favorite teachers spoke to me across the pages of books and in the flicker of a black-and-white television screen. When Andrew Carnegie funded libraries in small towns like mine, he knew about me. Books were luxuries my family could not afford, but at the Carnegie Library books were free . . . and to my six-year-old heart's delight children were allowed to borrow more than one at a time.[1]

The Carnegie was a primary source for learning, where personal teachers (books) resided and classrooms remained open after school. Subjects that interested me, music, art, history of England, American history, and the Italian Renaissance, turned into self-made courses of study. New ideas and information emerged throughout rows and rows of books that led to adventures across indefinite time to landscapes unknown.

Going up the stone stairs, through the massive oak doors, entering the Carnegie was magical. Its 1904 American Beaux-Arts architecture and interior were as transformative as the books inside. Dark wood, white marble pillars, a domed ceiling painted with flowing pastel images, and portraits of famous musicians circling the friezes in the great hall produced an ambience unlike any other place.[2] The touch of highly polished reading tables, plush, upholstered chairs, and the musty smell of old books beget lasting sensorial memories. It was a world apart, a sacred space, consecrated by imagination and inspiration, a temple of literacy.[3]

As with thousands of children and young people, my music education was enhanced by the live television broadcasts of the *Young People's Concerts* with Leonard Bernstein and the New York Philharmonic.[4] The orchestral performances in the great hall Carnegie built were available and admission was free. From 1958 to 1972, concerts inspired countless young listeners to become performers, music teachers and scholars, and dedicated audiences and patrons. As an educator, Leonard Bernstein was a master without equal. He possessed a deep passion for music, an all-consuming fire to teach, exemplary knowledge and skills, and a spiritual belief in the life-changing power of music.[5] He wrote:

> I've never stopped teaching. That's what I've always done, and have learned through teaching, one of the best ways I have of learning is from the people that I teach. All my television programs, there are almost a hundred scripts that I've written, are teaching, I even think of my conducting as teaching, in the sense that one is teaching one's vision of a piece to an orchestra and through them, to an audience. Anything that is sharing a feeling that one has or of knowledge which one may have, I don't go so far as to say wisdom, but anything which derives from the compulsion to share something one has, feels or knows, comes in the category of teaching. So that everything I do, really, is teaching.[6]

Volumes have been written about Bernstein and his immense accomplishments, but he was most proud of his achievements as a teacher. In the following narrative, Jamie Bernstein described her father's gifts:

> Bernstein's great gift was his ability to convey his own excitement about music. Watching him explain sonata form or the difference between a tonic and a dominant, you had the sense that he was letting you in on a wonderful secret, rather than drumming facts into you that might prove useful later. It doesn't matter what your subject is; a teacher's own passion is going to improve the student's ability to absorb and process the information. Excitement is contagious. . . . [It was] good luck that Leonard Bernstein and television came along at the same time. They were born for each other. (www.leonardbernstein.com)[7]

Bernstein taught music *with* music, not with lectures *about* music. He guided his listeners inside the experience of music and engaged them in a dialogue with music. In this particular exchange Bernstein demonstrated differences in timbre with selected instruments:

So what's the difference (in the sound) if I sing this?
Or play it on the piano (example) . . .
Or if the oboe plays it (example) . . .
Or the xylophone (example) . . .
Or the trombone (example) . . .
Very different. It's all the same note—only with a different sound. Now all music is a combination of sounds like that one.[8]

The orchestra was his musical instrument and teaching tool. In each concert, he called on the philharmonic to play examples from selected masterworks while he interjected salient points to guide the listeners. Every minute was tightly scripted and timed to meet the live broadcast schedule. With his audience prepared, the maestro conducted the selected work in its entirety. Considering this was a children's concert, the music and Bernstein's narrative were authentic, not reduced to trivia or oversimplified for children. Bernstein said that "talking down" to people you wish to engage ignores their "longing for insight and knowledge." Just as "talking up" with technical terms and concepts results in "losing contact." In the following excerpt, he summarizes music's meaning with profound depth of thought yet delivered through simple language:

> So you see, the meaning of music is in the music, in its melodies, and in the rhythms, and the harmonies, and the way it's orchestrated, and most important of all in the way it develops itself. But that's a whole other program. We'll talk about that some other time. Right now, all you have to know is that music has its own meanings, right there for you to find inside the music itself; and you don't need any stories or any pictures to tell you what it means. If you like music at all, you'll find out the meanings for yourselves, just by listening to it.
>
> So now, I want you to listen to a short piece without any explanation from anybody. I'm not going to tell you anything about it, except the name of it, and who wrote it. And you just all sit back and relax, and enjoy it, and listen to the notes, and feel them move around, jumping, and hopping, and bumping, and flashing, and sliding, and whatever they do, and just enjoy THAT without a whole lot of talk about stories and pictures and all that business. The piece we're going to play is by Ravel and is called "La Valse." I think you'll like it because it's fun to listen to and not for any other reason, not because it's about anything. It's just good, exciting music.

With that, he turned and conducted Ravel's *La Valse* with gesture and energy the music inspired. Bernstein's flamboyant conducting personified an intricate choreography of musical structure, melodic shape, rhythmic complexity, harmonic balance, instrumentation, tempo, and dynamics. The philharmonic's performance and Bernstein's conducting simultaneously enlivened the young audience and enriched their experience of music.

Bernstein knew his audience well. In the concert hall and at home, young people who themselves studied music, watched and listened attentively especially as youthful soloists performed. From 1960 to 1968, there were eight *Young People's Concerts* devoted to young performers. During those years, many future professional musicians debuted on live television with Bernstein and the New York Philharmonic:

Paul Green, clarinet, age thirteen
Heidi Lehwalder, harp, age fourteen
Lynn Harrell, cello, age sixteen
Elmar Oliveria, violin, age sixteen
Andre Watts, piano, age sixteen[9]
Horacio Guiterrez, piano, age seventeen
James Buswell, violin, age eighteen
Young Uck Kim, violin, age nineteen
Paula Robison, flute, age twenty
Gary Karr, double bass, age twenty
Veronica Tyler, soprano, age twenty-two
Harry Chapin was twelve years old when he narrated Benjamin Britten's *Young Person's Guide to the Orchestra*.

Premier conductors Aaron Copland, Seiji Ozawa (making his debut), Claudio Abbado, and Leopold Stokowski were invited to perform for these newly minted audiences. Until the advent of the Internet, equivalent performances were not available and free to so wide a young audience. Today, the Metropolitan Opera broadcasts live HDTV performances for an admission price at select theaters. In the United States, Public Broadcasting System (PBS) broadcasts *Live from Lincoln Center* and *Great Performances*, and for two seasons PBS offered *From the Top at Carnegie Hall*, starring young musicians with host Christopher Riley. However, none of these stellar programs surpasses the repertoire and musical experiences created specifically for children and young people of the *Young People's Concerts*, from 1958 to 1972.

Why this emphasis on Bernstein? Given his rock-star fame and unmatched musical accomplishments as performer, conductor, composer, and educator, he repeatedly claimed teaching as one of his greatest rewards, "Teaching is probably the noblest . . . most unselfish . . . most honorable profession in the world." He was a master communicator of and with music. In his distinctive style, he showed us new ways of thinking about music, studying, describing and analyzing, and performing and composing. Principles and attributes derived from Bernstein's writing, lecturing, and television programs inform those who study his work and inspire those who emulate his enthusiasm for learning. Each master teacher of music has qualities and characteristics in common, a dedication to teaching, passion for music and making music, belief in the life-changing power of music, and rigorous study of music and practice of musical skills.

LESSONS FROM THE *YOUNG PEOPLE'S CONCERTS*: IMPROVISATION

Have you ever heard a hundred-member symphony orchestra improvise? That's what happened when Bernstein asked the philharmonic to play without a score. To begin, he gave the downbeat for a solo instrument and directed the player's tempo and dynamics. Continuing, he cued entrances of soloists and sections; each player responded spontaneously and expressively as he or she created the rhythmic, melodic, and harmonic content of this symphonic improvisation. Not to be missed, the conductor and master teacher improvised and directed the structure, intensity, and spirit of the work to a thrilling finale. What an ingenious idea. If the conductor of the New York Phil could make this happen, so might a music teacher and his or her students freely improvise with rhythmic and melodic instruments—just like the mighty Phil. My instructions were brief and specific:

I'll be the conductor. Watch me.
I'll direct tempo and dynamics like this.
(Demonstration)
We will start with one instrument at a time.
I'll cue when it's your time to begin.
(Demonstration)
Keep performing as each instrument comes in.
(Demonstration)
When everyone's playing at the same time, watch for the cue to stop.
(Demonstration)
Now let's play it!

How much fun is *this*, just playing and making up music our way! Some music teachers have told me they are not comfortable or convinced that this spontaneous activity is "educational." Yet consider the learning objectives achieved here: *Creating* musical ideas; *playing* instruments; *listening* to other players; *imitating* and *applying* basic rules of *conducting*; *identifying, examining,* and *analyzing* music and its timbre, tempo and dynamics, rhythm and texture, form and structure.

In subsequent sessions, we found new ways of "how to make it better." Students experimented with different combinations of instruments, explored variations on tempo and dynamics, and took turns conducting. Each student conductor made a deliberate effort to create an original work unlike the others. Some of their improvisations led to full compositions, "Let's keep what we just did" and "Make a story out of it." We questioned whether everyone could remember what was played. "Everybody knows what *they* played." Another student said, "I know! Make a chart!" We gathered sheets of colored paper for each player to write his or her part. All the musical episodes were collected and spread across the classroom floor as a color-coded instrumental score. Students offered clever suggestions about "saving" and "writing down" their compositions, such as making audio or videotapes, pictures and doodles, and a graph "like sound waves."

Students eagerly suggested a variety of topics for music story making. "Let's make a hurricane," offered one third-grade student in my south Florida classroom. With agreement on this familiar topic, students invented a story line, improvised their ideas with instruments, and created a composition. This is how it began:

> *Great idea! Where and how does this storm begin?*
> (Student responses)
> *Where does it go, out to sea or hitting land?*
> (Student responses)
> *What sounds will it make, in the air, at sea, on land?*
> (Student responses)
> *What instruments do we need to tell the story's beginning-middle-end?*
> (Student responses)

This process continued until the class was ready to perform *Wilma, the Hurricane*.[10] "Again, let's do it again!"

What do you think is so exciting to children about experiences like this one? Of course, it's getting to play! Truly play, as in *playfulness* and the *play-spirit* that invites "let-me-do-it" individualism of young learners. When the play-spirit is embedded in music-making experiences, children's creativity is released and their interest, inspiration, and motivation to learn are assured. Working together with children in open and spontaneous activities requires attention to the essential balance between *freedom to create* and *need to know*. At each stage in the creative process, agreed-upon rules of procedure are essential to guide individuals and small groups of students and support optimum classroom conditions for learning and teaching. If creating and playing music are *the* most exciting things going on in the classroom, students stay engaged and focused on *learning*. Who wants to goof-off when playing music is more fun?

LISTENING TO MUSIC WITH IMAGINATION AND UNDERSTANDING

In each of fifty-three performances, the *Young People's Concerts* repertoire and musical explication delivered excellent lessons on compelling topics, for example:

- *What Is American Music?*
- *What Makes Music Symphonic?*
- *Humor in Music*
- *Who Is Gustav Mahler?*
- *What Is a Melody?*
- *Jazz in the Concert Hall*
- *Forever Beethoven*

- *Two Ballet Birds*

In the first concert, "What Does Music Mean?" parts of Modest Mussorgsky's *Pictures at an Exhibition* were performed by the young pianist Horacio Guiterrez. Following the piano performance, three guest conductors took the podium to introduce Maurice Ravel's colorful transcription for orchestra; Bernstein conducted the stunning finale, "The Great Gate of Kiev." Imagine hearing and comparing the original piano version and the Ravel orchestration of this exciting work, all in one concert, at once the same and different.[11]

Mussorgsky's exciting sonic paintings of his friend's art exhibition attract children's musical imagination of ballet chicks, a feisty witch, quirky gnomes, a mysterious castle, and a majestic city gate. "Promenade," the beginning and recurring theme, appeals to children's affinity for patterns in the repetitions of melodic content, rhythmic motifs, formal structure, phrases, and comparison of parts to the whole. In this instance, discovery, rather than direct instruction, favors the child's natural instincts for self-directed learning through his or her curiosity, imagination, open-mindedness, and liking for exploring and knowing. My introduction began as follows:

> *Listen to the way this music moves.*
> (Play a brief introduction)
> *Does this music walk, run, jog, skip, or jump?*
> (Play a brief example)
> (Discuss children's responses)
> *Listen again and let's try different ways to move.*
> (Select students one by one to perform)

After students explored ways to create musical gestures and movements, we examined what *inside* the music prompted their ideas. As children describe their perceptions, feelings, and thoughts at this time, teachers have opportunities to support children's ideas with corresponding musical vocabulary: rhythmic characteristics, regular and irregular beat, tempo changes, melodic events, shapes, and direction, parts and whole, patterns (same and not the same), repetition, variation, instrumentation, and expressivity. Asking children to memorize musical terms in the absence of music fails to achieve the intended goal.

Once my students experienced the piano and orchestral editions of *Pictures at an Exhibition,* we listened to Emerson, Lake, and Palmer's rock version and Animusic's digital animation of the finale. A word about Animusic: It was the first-of-its-kind music animation, designed by Wayne Lyle and his team. To showcase their innovative technology, Lyle's team created a breathtaking interpretation of "The Great Gate of Kiev," which they called "Cathedral Pictures." Their productions are distinctive because music drives the visuals, rather than the other way around when music serves as accompaniment or background. To date, Animusic's creators have produced two volumes and a third is in progress.

Children in my classroom were fascinated with each Animusic performance, especially "Pogo Sticks" and "Pipe Dream." Kids asked, parents phoned: "Where can I buy Animusic?" [12] Students' enthusiasm increased each time we watched the video on the big whiteboard. The synergy of music and image was intense: *"Look, this part is going to repeat. Watch the movement of patterns here and here. Now, this is where the tones quickly move upward. Hear it? See it?"* Through this digital mirror of music, children acquired yet another layer of powerful learning experiences. Multiple versions or treatments of the same work fasten musical impressions, layer upon layer, and are stored in children's minds for recall and reinvention, that is, knowledge applied.

The same principle of differing musical approaches holds true when teachers plan and teach children musical skills and conceptual precepts. Children and some adults like me have a restless curiosity for new ideas and a need for frequent changes of pace. Lessons that offer children diverse musical experiences heighten their interest, strengthen skills, stimulate sensitivity, and deepen understanding. Structure and discipline are placeholders for the true substance of all music lessons: listening to music, responding with gesture, movement, and dance, playing instruments, creating musical ideas, inventing music stories, writing and making music scores, and reading traditional and nontraditional notation of their own or others. [13]

Pictures at an Exhibition, Carnival of the Animals, and *Peter and the Wolf* [14] have compelling music and stories that children enjoy. Whether you choose to introduce the story line or the music first, the purpose of each lesson ought to be musical apprehension and understanding; specifically, "How does the composer make use of musical elements, qualities, and instruments to tell the story?" In a lesson that included Aaron Copland's *Billy the Kid,* the fourth-grade students were asked, "How many ways can you think of to tell a story?" Their answers were rich and imaginative: "You could . . ."

> *Write it in a book*
> *Tell it to someone*
> *Sing it*
> *Write it in a magazine or newspaper — a short story*
> *Paint it*
> *Make it into a movie*
> *Town crier tells it*
> *Puppets*
> *Conversation*

Play
Opera
Make it up
Use poetry
Dance
Make a list
In a speech
Through sign language
Cartoons
Comic books
Video games
Dreaming a story
Add to / adapt a story for young readers
Music can tell a story
Draw a poster
Items in a time capsule can tell a story
Mime
Touching a story for blind people
Photo story, a slide show
Musical percussion instruments
Write a story with no end and ask someone to finish
Sculpture—pottery
Cave drawings—markings
Sky-writing by airplane
Stars can tell stories like Greek myths
TV shows
Puzzles
Flags
Fire signals and totem poles
Bones and relics
Diorama
A charm bracelet
Graffiti
Quilt[15]

Students were lightning fast in their responses and vied with each other in an undeclared game for the most exceptional answers.[16] What a fountain of original, authentic music-teaching ideas, all generated by students. When students' contributions are valued and incorporated, their motivation to learn increases, and teachers benefit from their ideas.

The fourth-grade students discussed how we might connect "ways to tell a story" to music we previously studied. Someone suggested *time capsules*, collecting musical artifacts that represent our time for discovery by students in the distant future. Another idea was *bones and relics* "like that music from Halloween." They figured out the piece was *Danse maca-*

bre by Camille Saint-Saëns, the composer of the month for October. The student who said that quilts could tell a story remembered learning African-American freedom songs and stories: *Follow the Drinkin' Gourd* was about coded messages that guided slave people north to freedom. Another student explained that *drinkin' gourd* was code for the constellation the Big Dipper; and from whose two "pointer stars" opposite the handle direct the eye up to the North Star. We sang "The Gospel Train," "Swing Low Sweet Chariot," and "Little Red Caboose" and searched for hidden meaning in the lyrics: "home" meant a destination of a safe haven; "train and chariot" symbolized the Underground Railroad, and "over Jordan" referred to crossing the Ohio River to free states. Complementary to our songs, we read *Sweet Clara and the Freedom Quilt* (1993), a story of how women and girls sewed messages into patchwork quilts and hung them outside to warn of trouble, tell of plans for escapes, and depict maps to important points on the Underground Railroad.

Students said operas tell a story—you can sing a story, create a story with percussion instruments, and dance a story. The following lesson shows how music and dance tell stories. This begins one of my lessons on how music tells a story without words:

> *The composer who wrote the music we are learning today had a story line in mind. He's an American composer and his music sounds . . . well, American. You'll figure this out by listening to the first few bars. I'm not telling. It's for you to interpret. This is the way it begins . . .*

(Play opening from Copland's *Billy the Kid*)
Does this music give you a sense of time and place?
(Discussion)
There is a main (central) character represented by the music.
What is this character like?
(Play next excerpt)
(Discussion)
Let's join the orchestra.
What instruments do we have that we can play to match the percussion?
(Play next excerpt with students playing rhythmic accompaniments)

The first few bars of *The Open Prairie* prompted students' immediate responses: "It sounds like it's way out West." Throughout *Billy the Kid*, Copland orchestrated songs that students recognized as cowboy music even though they could not identify any of the pieces by name. "I just know it . . ." After hearing the old American songs in *Billy the Kid*, students were eager to learn them, "Git Along Little Dogies," "The Old Chisholm Trail," and "Goodbye Old Paint." Unlike conventional methods that call for teaching the songs before the orchestral versions, this approach let Copland's brilliant orchestration introduce the songs. His orchestral treatments of the songs are exciting, vivid, and memorable.

Once students were familiar with Copland's music, they listened for new clues to further unravel the musical story of the famous outlaw.

Imagine students' surprise when they found out that *Billy the Kid* is a classical ballet. Given kids' sense of humor, they made all sorts of comments about cowboys in tights and tutus. When the hilarity died down, I explained that not all components of ballets—the music, story, costumes, and sets—were created in the same style. Boys and girls alike knew *The Nutcracker* as performers or audience members. On the occasion of Tchaikovsky's birthday, we played music from *Swan Lake*. Several children said, "I know that from Disney." In subsequent sessions, students watched scenes from *Swan Lake* performed by the American Ballet Theatre. Students were familiar with *The Nutcracker's* Christmas setting, costumes, and dancing children, toys, candies, and sweets; however to them, *Swan Lake* was dark and otherworldly. Here are some of their curious questions and comments:

> *Why don't they talk?*
> *Can't they talk?*
> *Are they clones?*
> *They are all exactly the same!*
> *Is this for real?*
> *Are they real people?*
> *Is this animation?*
> *What's a swan?*
> *Are they swans?*
> *One time my Mom faded [fainted] like the Queen.*
> *I really like Swamp Guy [Rothbart].*

Many wanted to know why the men didn't wear "pants," and why the women had such "big" feet. We talked about why different types of shoes are needed: "No shoes if you're swimming," "tennis shoes," "running shoes," "soccer players' shoes have cleats," "Tap dancers' shoes." Discussion was lively and suggestions endless. Firmly convinced that special shoes are designed for particular actions and movement, we returned to the question of ballet shoes for women and men. Following my descriptions and demonstrations of shoes, we watched, in slow motion and freeze-frames, women poised and spinning in pointe shoes and men leaping and landing in shoes of soft leather. Even a brief activity such as this opened children's eyes and minds to music and ballet that otherwise they might not have experienced. As students prepared to exit, they tiptoed to the door: "See, I can do it too."

My students knew lots of music, songs, and instrumental music from movies, television, video games, Disney soundtracks, and even music at Disney World's theme parks. The Wilderness Lodge Resort plays an impressive selection of Western-themed instrumental music in the lobby and common areas, including selections from Copland's *Rodeo* and *Billy the Kid.* Children might not have previous knowledge of the music, but upon hearing the same music again, they recognize it and remember where they heard it. Context, circumstance, and settings influence each child's experience of music. By acknowledging this musical experience, teachers acquire yet another effective instructional strategy. At the first hearing of Mozart's *Eine kleine Nachtmusik*, students wildly waved their hands for recognition. "It's the Lexus commercial!" To be sure, a local movie theater ran commercials before the feature film—there it was— Mozart selling Lexus automobiles. It's always good to know what music they know; just ask, "Where did you hear it?"

DISCOVERING MUSIC THROUGH ANIMATION

Students in my elementary school were experts on Disney music from *Snow White*, reissues of 1937, to *Frozen* (2013). From the outset, Disney hired the best contemporary songwriters and composers to work for him. (One famous composer asked, "Walt who?") Many well-loved and award-winning songs were composed by Sammy Fain and Sammy Cahn (*Peter Pan*); Sonny Burke (*Cinderella, Alice in Wonderland*); Alan Menken (*The Little Mermaid; Beauty and the Beast*); Robert and Richard Sherman (*Mary Poppins, The Jungle Book*); Randy Newman (*Toy Story; Monsters, Inc.; The Princess and the Frog*); and Michael Giacchino (*UP; The Incredibles; Ratatouille*). Having developed brilliant innovations in animation technology, Walt Disney created his third major animated film, *Fantasia*, through which he popularized baroque, classical, romantic, and twentieth-century music for generations of children yet to come. Eminent musician and music advocate for children Leopold Stokowski[17] conducted *Fantasia* with the Philadelphia Orchestra for a family audience who watched these great masterworks come alive in animation on a movie screen. In 1940, for the first time, a musical score and its musical elements were synchronized with moving images, enhanced by colorful visuals, and presented using both abstract and programmatic images. *Fantasia*'s ambitious concert program included works by Bach (Toccata and Fugue in D Minor), Tchaikovsky (*The Nutcracker Suite*), Dukas (*The Sorcerer's Apprentice*), Stravinsky (*Rite of Spring*), Beethoven (excerpts from the *Pastoral Symphony*), Ponchielli's ("Dance of the Hours"), Mussorgsky (*Night on Bald Mountain*), and Franz Schubert ("Ave Maria").

Roy E. Disney, Walt's nephew, coproduced *Fantasia 2000* with James Levine and the Chicago Symphony. The new *Fantasia* premiered at Carnegie Hall and continued on a concert tour in five cities. Afterwards, the film had an IMAX viewing and for several months it was shown in local movie theaters. Disney's advanced computer-generated animation technology brought about a magical masterpiece in *Fantasia 2000*. The repertoire included: Beethoven, Symphony No. 5, Allegro con brio;

Gershwin, *Rhapsody in Blue*; Shostakovich, Piano Concerto No. 2 in F major, Allegro; Saint-Saëns, *Carnival of the Animals*, Finale; Elgar, *Pomp and Circumstance*, Marches 1, 2, 3, and 4; and Stravinsky, *The Firebird Suite*. The only work from *Fantasia 1940* remastered for *Fantasia 2000* was Mickey's *Sorcerer's Apprentice*.

Whenever the *Sorcerer* was played, kids donned Mickey the Sorcerer's pointy hats and conjured up broom magic for thematic effects. They knew the musical theme for the sorcerer's magic spell and followed it throughout the composition. In one lesson we listened to the upwardly spiraling melodic motif that symbolized water rapidly rising and overflowing. "Oh no!" the children shouted, "Here comes some more!" They recognized the musical counterpoint as each broom splintered into multiple clones. At the end of the lesson, I asked the students (expecting answers about music), "So, what did you learn?" Students replied, "Do what you're TOLD!"

DISCOVERING MUSIC THROUGH OPERA

Ballet and opera are genres that few teachers are willing to approach. You understand why. For many years TV commercials have exploited operatic singing to sell one product or another. The singers sing dreadfully and look ridiculous. Children wanted to know:

> *Why do they sing that way?*
> *It's like the Olympics of singing.*
> *While most of us can run, cycle, swim, and play summer and winter games,*
> *Olympians are exceptional performers and players at their sport.*
> *All of us can sing, but opera singers are exceptional*
> *in talent, training, and performance.*

One of my most rewarding music lessons focused on music's meaning in an operatic aria. The intent was not about opera stories or how singers train their voices, but about the heartfelt emotion in the singing. We listened to Mirella Freni's performance of "Un bel di" from Puccini's *Madame Butterfly*, in three parts: Part 1, recitative, Part 2, lyrical section, and Part 3, dramatic conclusion. "What do you think she's feeling as she sings?" The children responded with tender sensitivity and acute perception:

Part 1:

> *She's feeling hopeless.*
> *She's feeling betrayed.*

Part 2:

She's remembering her childhood.
Her past is sad.
Someone died.
She is worried.

Part 3:

She wants to fight back for what she did wrong.
She feels guilty.
She is sorry.
She has her hope back.
She believes in herself.
She is ready for the future.
She has the courage to do something.
She is peaceful.

Amazing, isn't it? Would you be surprised to know that these students were seven to eight years old and in second grade? How could such young children respond knowingly to the emotion of the music and the singer's expressivity? My expectations were embarrassingly below their depth of apprehension and sensitivity. [*Note to self: Do not underestimate children's musical sensibilities.*] Their classroom teachers were surprised to learn that boys and girls responded with equal interest and understanding: "I wouldn't think *any* of them would listen to opera." Before and during the lesson, children were not aware of *Madama Butterfly*'s story nor did they understand the words sung in Italian. At the children's request, we listened a second time without interruption. At the last note's silence, a thoughtful child predicted, "She has the courage to do something." It was not appropriate to share what Butterfly had the courage to do, but they sensed the emotion without knowledge of the impending tragedy.

How *music feels is what it means* to you, to me, and especially to children.[18]

PLAYING WITH MOZART

Children love Mozart. They often listened, sang, conducted, and accompanied Mozart's music with instruments. Some of their favorite compositions were: Variations on "Ah! vous dirai-je, maman" (we know it as the tune of "Twinkle, Twinkle Little Star"), Turkish March, *Eine kleine Nachtmusik*, overture to *The Marriage of Figaro*, overture to *The Magic Flute*, and Symphony no. 40 in G Minor, first movement. Students said, "I think I heard that on Tom and Jerry" and "I know that. It's on my baby brother's Mozart video."

Mozart Children on Tour

Mozart's young life as composer and performer intrigued children. They were amazed to learn that Mozart's father, Leopold Mozart, took his two young children on concert tours for more than four years. Wolfgang was six years old and his sister, Maria Anna (Nannerl), was ten years old when they left home to perform in eighty-eight cities at royal courts and palaces throughout Europe and across the English Channel to London. The children received unmatched accolades, royal gifts, and honors for their outstanding performances; Wolfgang played violin and Nannerl, the piano. Students asked me about Mozart's sister, "Was she famous?" Nannerl was a very talented child and loved her little brother. They were very close as children. They played music together and created an imaginary kingdom where they were king and queen and spoke a secret language they invented. Before age eighteen she continued to perform and was considered one of Europe's finest pianists. Letters to and from her famous brother showed that she composed music. However, none of her compositions survived.

We playacted these and other stories about young Mozart and his music. We improvised scenes and took on roles of Papa Mozart, Nannerl, Mama Mozart, and various musicians in his young life. Students loved one particular story about Mr. Schachtner. When Papa Mozart refused young Wolfgang permission to join his rehearsals, Mr. Schachtner kindly asked if the little boy might sit by him and play his child-size violin. Everyone, especially Papa Mozart, was astounded at the child's brilliant playing. My young students identified with the parent-child conflict: "See! He could do it!" "They'll let him play next time!"

The video series *Mozart on Tour*, with André Previn as narrator, conductor, and pianist, contains thirteen episodes of documentary reenactments of Mozart's life and music. When children viewed scenes of Mozart's early years, they were transported to his time and place.

"What did you notice about the difference in Mozart's time and our time?" The children answered with keen observations and deductions:

They had candles for lights.
Different clothes and shoes
Wigs
Horses and buggies
Men wore high heels.
No computers and TV back then
Or iPhones, iPads, iPods
Kids dressed up.
. . . like grown-ups.
They didn't play sports.
. . . go to movies.

Mozart didn't go to school.

Mozart Tells a Story

Students' enthusiasm for everything Mozart provided an effective transition to a challenging lesson on "How Mozart tells a story with orchestral music, singers, dancers, costumes, and scenery—on a big stage." "Does anyone know what we call a music-storytelling performance like this?" "OPRAH!" Hmmm—after we sorted out the differences between "Oprah" and "opera," students enjoyed the play on words and always got a laugh with, "Are we watching Oprah today?" Sharing children's penchant for humor brings about classroom conditions for playful learning in a happy atmosphere. My students delighted in this introduction to *The Magic Flute*:

> *Today, we're going to study an "Oprah" by Mozart.*
> NO, you mean Opera!
> *What do you mean? Is there a difference?*
> Oprah's a TV show!
> *Oh yes, I do mean an OPERA by Mozart. I think you'll like it. It has an evil queen.*
> *Do you know any stories with evil queens?*

Children relished the chance to identify familiar baddies:

> *There's one in Sleeping Beauty.*
> *. . . Maleficent!*
> *. . . She made the Princess go to sleep until the Prince kissed her awake.*
> *I had my picture made with the one that said, "Who is the fairest of them all?"*
> *. . . Snow White's mother.*
> *. . . No, stepmother.*
> *. . . She changed into a witch and gave her a poison apple.*
> *Ursula. She was in The Little Mermaid.*
> *. . . She's a Sea Witch and takes Ariel's voice.*
> *. . . I don't know if she's a queen.*
> *A witch is in Hansel and Gretel, but she's not a queen.*
> *And Cruella de Vil—she's not a queen, but she's evil.*

During our discussion, I showed pictures and film clips of several "evil ones." The visuals piqued the children's interest in the music and the questions increased their participation:

> *What evil things did she do?*
> *What made her do it?*
> *What did she want that she did not have?*

Did she have any evil helpers?
Did she look evil? Did she have an evil voice?
Let's listen to her song. What does the music tell about what she's like?

After we pondered the evil ways of the Disney characters, played instruments, danced and sang some of their signature songs, we were ready for Mozart's Evil Queen.

In Mozart's opera The Magic Flute *there is an*
evil queen called The Queen of the Night.
Let's listen to her.
(Musical example)
What in her singing tells you she's an evil queen?

Few, if any, children in my school had ever heard the pyrotechnical coloratura singing of anyone like the Queen of the Night. Nonetheless, they accepted her singing as the *message* about her evildoing. This is some of what they said about the Evil Queen of the Night:

She sounds angry at somebody.
She is REALLY loud.
If she's the Queen of the Night, she stays in the dark. That makes her mad.
Her face is evil. She has long fingernails.
Her high notes make her sound angry too.
I explained: *Yes, she is angry. The Queen of the Night was furious because she had been deprived of her power, so she swears revenge and plans to harm her daughter if she does not obey her.*
One child said, *That's like Maleficent!*
Another said, *And Ursula!*

It was truly gratifying that my students showed exceptional interest in *The Magic Flute.* We enjoyed many characters and events, especially a funny scene when Papageno and Tamina were captured and endangered by Monostatos and his men. One excited child shouted out to Papageno, "Use your bells. Use your stupid bells!" Julie Taymor's costumes, sets, and fantastical puppets added magic to Mozart's enchanting, unforgettable music. After viewing the DVD, the students immediately said, "Let's see it again."

MUSIC IN CONTEXT: SETTING THE SCENE

Visuals, film, still photographs, costumes,[19] artifacts, and props may be used successfully to connect children with music of a particular historical era, geographical region, and fantastic worlds of make believe. Used as prompts, such items capture students' attention and invite conjecture. Younger students perked up at, "Once upon a time . . ." or "Long ago and far away . . ." Older students showed interest in music and topics for time and place: "In the Time of Knights and Castles," "Pirates and Sailing Ships," "George Washington," and "Freedom Songs from Abraham Lincoln to Martin Luther King Jr." There are as many ways to explore, as there are songs and composition. Placing music in its historical and cultural contexts strengthens the students' immediate experience and opens windows for future learning. In this instance, you may wish to introduce the music first and invite the children's ideas afterwards:[20]

Who might have been the first people who listened to this music?
Can you imagine where they heard it?
Was this now or a time long ago?
How would you describe this music to someone who'd never heard it?

MUSICAL CONNECTIONS

Of all the traditional holidays, Thanksgiving seems to be the most celebrated in elementary school and least likely to generate controversy. Children learn that the Pilgrims "gave thanks" for a bountiful harvest; and that Squanto, an English-speaking American Indian, befriended the Pilgrims. Squanto acted as their interpreter and he taught them to plant corn, where and how to hunt and fish. In preparation for music lessons involving history and culture, be sure to know the facts, conditions, and music authentic to the time and place.

In a series of lessons titled *Music in the Time of Early Americans: The Pilgrims*, I asked students in second grade, "Who can tell us something about the Pilgrims?" This is what they said:

Squanto was the first one to visit them.
Pilgrims were searching for a New World.
They sailed on the Mayflower from England.
There were 102 passengers.
It took sixty-six days.
They got sick.
They had to stand on their knees because it was so crowded.
One person died.
One baby was born.
Forty-six people died after the first winter.
They brought seeds and dry meat.
They ate hardtack and dried cheese.
They carried water in old, wood barrels. The water went bad and made them sick.
They brought tools.

They brought pillows and blankets.
They brought cradles.
They brought clothes.
They did not bring toys for children. There was not enough room on the ship.

"Did the Pilgrims know any music?" I asked. "No," they replied. Students thought it was too long ago and the Pilgrims didn't know how to make music. Otherwise the children were knowledgeable, interested, focused, and ready to discover music the Pilgrims knew. For these lessons, there are wonderful children's songs, rounds, street cries, dances, and processionals from a book compiled by John Langstaff, *A Revels Garland of Song: In Celebration of Spring, Summer & Autumn.* Every song in this collection is a treasure:

"One Man Shall Mow My Meadow" is an English cumulative song about the harvest. It is a beautiful song for children's voices and lends itself to a simple choreography with dancers mowing, shearing, and gathering hay. When singing and dancing are synchronized, children can actually hear and see the song's structure.

"High! Ho! The Rattlin' Bog" is another English cumulative song with many variants, such as the well-known "Greenwood Tree." These songs contain numerous stanzas (six in this one) and are referred to as "the everlasting circle." The introduction reads, "This version was collected by the great Irish piper and traditional singer Seamus Ennis in Dublin." As true of songs passed down, around, and across generations and geographical regions, the lyrics change, the melodies change, and some songs leave the pubs and go on to polite company. The same tune for "Rattlin' Bog" was used in a drinking song, "The Barley Mow." [*Note to self: Be careful of barley songs, always read the lyrics carefully.*]

"Oats and Beans and Barley Grow" is a delightful children's singing game about a farmer planting, tending, and harvesting crops. We created a variation on the game described in John Langston's book. We sang and mimed the actions about planting in the first part of the song. Boys and girls mime the actions according to the lyrics. In the second part of the song, the farmers sing with gusto about the easy (lazy) life of farming. Next all sweetly sing, "Waiting for a partner." Suspicious about the farmers' intent, the girls set out the rules for husbands, singing: "Now that you're married, you must obey, you must be true to all you say; You must be wise, you must be good, and help your wife to chop the wood!" The girls added their own indignation, shouting, *"Chop the WOOD?"* The tune is from Shropshire and thought to be part of an English country dance.

"The May Day Carol" is one of the loveliest songs in the collection. It has always been revered as a springtime carol when loved ones, friends, and children placed flowers at doorsteps early on the morning of the first

day of May. This variant, collected in Bedfordshire by Annie Gilchrist, is
my favorite:

> A branch of May I bring you here,
> And at your door I stand,
> It's nothing but a sprout,
> but it's well budded out by the work of God's own hand.

"The Helston Furry" is a springtime processional dance celebrated by
generations of villagers of Helston, in Cornwall on May 8. They dressed
in costumes, carried flowers and garlands of flowers, and sang and
danced throughout the village, in the streets and in and out of houses
opened for the celebration.

"Great Tom Is Cast" is a simple round that refers to the six-ton Tom
bell cast in 1680 for Christ Church Oxford.

"Strawberry" and "New Mussels" are seventeenth-century English
street cries. These and similar ones may be used to invite children's solo
singing and prompt improvisations and composed street cries of their
own.

The kindergarten children did not believe that Pilgrims had music,
either. "Why didn't they have music?" These five-year-olds answered
with firm conviction:

No electricity.
No CDs.
No metal.
No batteries.
No TV.
No instruments.
No computers.
No radio stations.
No toys.
They didn't know how to sing.
Only girls knew how to sing. Boys didn't.

A subsequent series of thematic lessons, Music in the Time of Early
Americans: The American Indians, comprised songs, chants, drums,
dances, and legends unique to the Indian nations of the eastern coastal
regions and the western plains.

Students in first grade did not believe American Indians had music.
"Why didn't they have music?"

They didn't build any.
They didn't understand music.
They didn't know how to make instruments.
They didn't know how to sing.

They didn't like to sing.
They didn't know how to make notes.
They didn't know about instruments.

Few of my youngest Florida students knew names of American Indians, except Seminoles. They were fascinated to learn names of many other tribes through Ella Jenkins's song and chant "We Are Native American Tribes." We learned the song and created our own classroom performance. First, I divided the students into three performing groups: One group sang and chanted; the second performed a simple stylized dance; and the third group provided accompaniment with drums, rattles, and bells. The children were rotated until all performed in each group.

Students in a second-grade class learned about Squanto and how he helped the Pilgrims survive their first winter. They learned Squanto's story through a CD recording, *Squanto and the First Thanksgiving*, performed by Graham Greene as storyteller and with music created by Paul McCandless. After we discussed events in the story, I asked, "How does music help tell this story?" The children answered thoughtfully:

It helps you travel back in time.
Helps the storyteller tell with emotion.
Helps you imagine that it really happened.
Helps make the story in our heads.
Helps people remember the story because there were no books back then.

FINAL THOUGHTS ON REPERTOIRE AND RESOURCES

There is no single, ready-made bank of music-teaching ideas; each teacher must develop his or her own. Music educators have hundreds of sources from which to choose materials, online, in grade-level music texts, children's books, at workshops, and recommendations by word of mouth. So many choices can be overwhelming; therefore, I suggest that you first examine the music you already know. Your lifetime experience of music is your wellspring of music best known and most meaningful. All such works are a part of your active repertoire: music you have studied, performed, heard in concert, saved in your music library, and playlisted on your digital devices. By searching a personal inventory, you will find songs and instrumental works applicable for students you teach. As you begin to inventory and categorize your collected works, you may discover you know more music than you realize. Next, think of those music teachers who inspired you and those whose knowledge and techniques were exceptionally effective and worth emulating.

These steps will guide you to seek music and materials that provide novelty and stimulate children's curiosity. Proceed then to involve students in the moment, make the lessons lively, and above all, enjoy your work. The best teaching is improvisatory. Plan and teach like a jazz musician: Know the musical structure; memorize the content, practice, and play.

FOLLOW THE CHILDREN

What does the learning child reveal that teachers most need to know? In their habitat, children are social actors in their own realm; they are spontaneous by nature, and boundlessly curious and expressive. From first light, they seek novelty, excitement, and funny stuff. Children are imaginative and ingenious players in a world of their making. Do not be misled. The child's mind is not a blank slate or empty vessel waiting to be filled with information or a computer in need of programming. Neither does the child's mind operate as if it were a compartmentalized file or card catalog. The child we teach, parent, and care for is a loving child, a sensitive and moral child, a physical and growing child, a thinking and reasoning child, a creating and playing child . . . a whole child.

NOTES

1. Although his business practices were not always most admirable, Andrew Carnegie built more than three thousand libraries worldwide. His philanthropy created Carnegie Hall, Carnegie Institutes, Carnegie Foundations, Carnegie Endowment for International Peace, Carnegie Museums for art, history, and the sciences, universities, hospitals, churches, and public parks. Before he died, Carnegie gave away a fortune "for the good of my fellow men [and] to continue to benefit humanity."

2. Most likely, there were portraits of scientists and inventors, historians and philosophers that I no longer recall. To my chagrin, *my* Carnegie Library building was demolished to make way for a new county library, so bleak and uninspiring.

3. Mary B. Dierickx, *The Architecture of Literacy: The Carnegie Libraries of New York City*. New York: Cooper Union for the Advancement of Science and Art and the New York City Dept. of General Services, 1996; and Theodore Jones, *Carnegie Libraries across America: A Public Legacy*. Washington, DC: Preservation Press, 1997.

4. *Young People's Concerts*, DVDs, vols. 1, 2, also available on YouTube.

5. Few of my college courses in music literature, history, and theory inspired or informed my youthful zeal for learning music. Would that my Theory 2 professor had played a bit of Bach to introduce the rules of counterpoint instead of approaching this brilliant technique like a sonic puzzle for his students to solve. Maybe it's different now . . .

6. *ASCAP Today*, May 1972.

7. Jamie Bernstein, *Leonard Bernstein: A Born Teacher*. http://www.leonardbernstein.com.

8. *Young People's Concerts*, "What Does Music Mean?" January 18, 1958.

9. In March 2000, I met Andre Watts after his performance with the Atlanta Symphony conducted by music director Yoel Levi. "Mr. Watts, I've met you before!" I said. Surprised and gracious, he asked me to remind him. "Actually, it was when I watched your debut with Leonard Bernstein on a live broadcast of the *Young People's Concerts*." He was delighted. Over dinner, we talked at length about his experiences as a young performer. Neither of us could remember the "long, long ago" performance date. Afterwards, I checked the concert schedule and found that Andre had performed the

Liszt Concerto No. 1 for Orchestra and Piano in E-flat on January 15, 1963; and, four years later, he played the Brahms Piano Concerto No. 2 in B-flat Major on the Young Performer's Alumni concert, April 19, 1967.

10. Hurricane Wilma, October 24, 2005, roared through the Gulf Coast across to southeast Florida. Schools in some areas were closed for two weeks.

11. Mussorgsky, *Pictures at an Exhibition* (Original Piano Version & Orchestral Version: Ashkenazy) by Modest Mussorgsky, Vladimir Ashkenazy, and Philharmonia Orchestra of London (1990).

12. See www.animusic.com.

13. Under No Child Left Behind and Race to the Top, states and local school districts require standardized music lessons with a single objective, few activities, and limited repertoire, contrary to what is necessary for children's optimum development.

14. Picture books with audio CDs are available for each of these works.

15. Not only did they exceed my expectations, their ideas were far better and more numerous than mine.

16. Similarly, students delighted in being first to identify a musical selection. Within three to five seconds, they recognized themes from the *Star Wars* movies, *Indiana Jones*, *Jaws*, a few more seconds for *Superman, E.T.*, and video game scores.

17. See Leopold Stokowski and the Pillsbury Studies.

18. In an introduction to a lovely guitar solo, "Carrying You" by Larry Carlton from his album, *Alone, but Never Alone*, the children were asked to move in response to "how the music feels to you." As they listened, made gestures and movement, I led and followed them. Afterwards, I asked, "What was it like [their experiences of listening and moving]?" Not only does this experience reveal children's knowledge of *music*; it reveals knowledge of *the children*. These were the images they described:

"Night . . . looking at the stars; they bring light into your mind."
"It's a marriagey-lovey song."
"Picking roses and giving them to someone."
"Fairy dust—making people's wishes come true."
"Someone died; you were thinking about the good times."
"Seeing light—after being scared."
"Picking oranges and squeezing the juice into people's cup."
"Daydreaming—like being in a dream world."
"Shooting stars—trying to catch them."
"Secret garden music."
"How you feel after something hard that you did."
"Swimming in the river."
"Finding gold and giving it to poor people."
"In the fall, picking up leaves and tossing them up."
"Finding water and splashing it over people."

19. My collection of costumes, or as the children called them, "your dress-up clothes," added visual interest to my lessons, African dashiki, Japanese *yukata*, colonial boy's three-cornered hat, shirt, and sash, and Renaissance garb.

20. Examples: *Star Wars, The Empire Strikes Back, Return of the Jedi, Indiana Jones, E.T.*, and *Jaws*.

TWO

Imagination

The Musical Culture of Children's Play

On the seashore of endless worlds, children play.
—Rabindranath Tagore

"Let's play!" These are the happiest two words of childhood. Whether playing music, soccer, games with rules, or free play without rules, children and some adults are at their creative and personal best at play. I believe in play. It is the birthplace of curiosity, imagination, creativity, and the cradle of children's social and cognitive development.

Children's play is complex, illusive, fleeting, and difficult to define. Nonetheless, child development and play scholars and researchers agree that play is voluntary, enjoyable, active, without extrinsic goals, and absent adult intervention. Children may engage in playing freely alone, with others, or independently, yet side by side. Contemporary research demonstrates that play contributes to children's comprehensive development, socially, knowing self and others, emotionally, feeling and expression, and intellectually, thinking, imagining, and inventing.

Children play with music. On their own or with others, they make up spontaneous songs, improvise dance moves, and play at rhythm making, often all at the same time with props, costumes, and toys. The playscape is likely to be outside the presence or beyond the attention of adults: "The four-year-old passed the time by singing made-up-on-the-spot songs, dancing around, and trying to catch her parent's attention. Happily, she created her own amusement with self-made music while her parent was otherwise engaged" (Littleton, 1998).

Examples of children's spontaneous song and dance like this one just described are often seen but rarely regarded seriously, observed systematically, or preserved for further study. One remarkable exception con-

25

cerns the work directed by Lori Custodero, "Tunes and Rhythms as Transitional Objects: Children's Spontaneous Musical Behaviors in the Subway" (2014).[1]

PROBLEM SEEKING: THE PLAY FACTOR

Having observed children at play with music in various settings, including prekindergarten classrooms, unanswered questions emerged: (a) How might children play with music if given opportunity and free time? (b) How might traditional, teacher-directed lessons in music for young children incorporate opportunities for free play? (c) What setting might provide a favorable environment to observe and study children at play with music?

In 1978 I volunteered to develop a music program for Head Start and teach a class of three-year-olds at a Child Development Center in a small, southeastern Tennessee town. Several visits were necessary to get to know the children and ease into their surroundings. But the first time they met me in a circle-time music activity, they recoiled. Most of the seventeen children quietly turned away from eye contact, others were decidedly adverse to my invitations to sing, play small percussion, or even clap hands. What was wrong? Their teacher explained that few of these children knew anyone outside their families, and even though a frequent visitor, I was still a stranger to them. What to do? Is it possible to approach the children indirectly? Ventriloquism? No. What about a double, a doppelgänger? Yes. My daughter's Raggedy Ann doll, about the size of a three-year-old with a friendly smile, was a perfect fit to sit in my lap with her face forward toward the children and mine hidden behind. Success! From that day forward, Raggedy Ann went to preschool. With her happy face, moveable arms and legs, she engaged the shy children with songs and movement: *Clap, clap, clap your hands, clap your hands together* led to many verses such as *Tap your toes, touch your nose, nod your head*. Children responded to "If You're Happy and You Know It, Clap Your Hands," "This Old Man," "The Itsy Bitsy Spider," "Hush, Little Baby," and similar songs for young children. In the same manner, they responded to audio recordings of children's songs from Disney movies and selected classical instrumental music. Raggedy Ann learned to hold jingle bells, shakers, rattles, and play rhythms along with the recorded music.

Over time, when the children comfortably adjusted to Raggedy Ann, she moved to sit beside me instead of in my lap. With the children comfortably sitting in a semicircle, it seemed appropriate to introduce a small hand drum to each child, one at a time. "Would you like to play it?" The first few children would not touch the drum. Moving on to the next child and to the next, I tried another approach. Without speaking to the child, I placed it on the floor and tapped the drum. Finally a little girl placed her hand on the drum. She paused, looked at me, and to my surprise, she tapped the drum, just once, as I did. Our delightful game was afoot. We played the drum upside down and right side up, we rubbed and scratched the surface; we walked and ran two-legged fingers around the edge, and played with two hands at once. Children responded and imitated challenging rhythms, changes in dynamics, louder to softer, and tempo faster to slower. The shy little girl followed me precisely each time it was her turn. Then she created the new best game in town! Playfully, *she* began to lead me. Her intentional responses confirmed that we had established a meaningful, playful, and musical dialogue. Each child whose turn came after understood the game from watching her. Instantly, others asked to play too, including those who had earlier refused. Be mindful that these three-year-olds' reluctance to participate in this new activity with a new object was not unfounded. After the session, their teacher told me why the children were unwilling to play. She said that even the tuning keys on the hand drum may have discouraged some children's participation; "It looks unsafe . . . to them." The children taught me to follow, not lead, and listen to them, not talk.

OBSERVATIONAL STUDIES: FREE PLAY WITH MUSIC

Unobtrusive video recordings documented each music session. Playback of the drum session (described above) showed that these children produced eighteen unique responses on the drum. In some instances, they copied each other; but it was remarkable that they created so many different rhythmic ideas. Curiosity at this finding invited a replication with non-musician adults.[2] Results showed that they were less inventive with the same drum improvisation activity than the group of three-year-olds.

For ten months, during the 1978/1979 school year, my schedule included weekly music visits to the same group of children in the same setting. In each session, teacher-guided experiences took priority over teacher-directed activities. It was of utmost importance to find a way to guide very young children's attention to music without telling them about the music. Would they listen, attend, and respond to music unless directed to "follow me?" Discovering and knowing children's instinctive response to music, not merely their mimicked response to my directives, was the greatest challenge in my teaching years. Music in preschool for young children, at that time, consisted of rote-learned songs and not-so-musical recordings about colors, numbers, and actions, with narratives such as "stand up, sit down, brush your teeth," and "march" to programmed directions.

Only the *best* music is *best* for children and other living things. "Grown-up" art music is often played quietly as background for rest or nap time. But how might teachers engage young children in a more absorbing musical experience? Consider Vivaldi's *Four Seasons*, specifically the slow-movement section of "Winter" for this untried learning event. The violin solo is exquisite, but would the children react to music they'd never heard before, especially an eighteenth-century baroque violin concerto? You already suspect my answer is "yes," but how this good result was achieved may surprise.

Picture this: There are seventeen three-year-olds and me lying on our backs looking up at the ceiling, classroom lights dimmed. With a flashlight aimed at the ceiling, I asked the children to point at the spot of light and follow it as it moved around. Intently, they pointed at the light and followed the patterns of circles and lines on the ceiling. After they rested a bit, the children were prepared to hear the violin solo in the slow movement of Vivaldi's "Winter." As the music began, I reset the spotlight and asked the young children to point and follow the light as it moved across the ceiling. Due to my control of the spotlight, the children's experience of music corresponded to what they felt and heard, simultaneously, with the slowly moving tempo of the violin solo. With the beacon of light as guide, I tracked the contour and the structure of the melodic phrases. As each phrase began and ended, I changed the direction of the spotlight, and copied rhythm patterns for their eyes and ears with zigzag lines and bouncing spots. Smaller to larger circles indicated dynamic volume. As they looked at the ceiling "way up high," they listened for the high sounds. The patterned movement of the light created a visual choreography of the music as they heard it in real time. The videotape playback showed that the episode lasted 5:10 minutes and that one child, the little girl who led the drum improvisations, held on and on through a lengthy fermata on the last note until the sound disappeared. Spellbound with the power of musical attraction, the children were no less enthralled than an adult audience captivated by a concert performance. Young children's musical perception must not be undervalued. They know more than they can tell.[3]

Similar learning experiences encouraged children's rich response and eager involvement. Their interest encouraged me to offer more time for play. As each lesson came near to a close, the children were invited to play with the music instruments, puppets, children's music books, picture books, and other teaching materials previously introduced. Quietly I scattered the materials about and refrained from initiating play, interrupting, or intervening, unless invited. One by one, children picked up an instrument, puppet, or book that interested them. They played alone, side by side, and in small groups. Often children played with an instrument or musical material exactly as we had played with it during the lesson. At other times, they engaged each other with ideas of their own:

> One of the children chose a picture book with musical notation and sat
> down beside me. Without a word, she opened the book and turned the

pages at random. We looked together and after a while I asked, "Do you know this song?" She confidently replied, "Yes." "How do you think it goes?" Rather than tell me, as I expected, she sang a made-up-on-the-spot song while rhythmically pointing to the pictures and music notation. She continued turning pages, singing, and incorporating the picture stories in the verbal content of her songs. This child's improvised rhythms fell regularly within a steady pulse, in discernible phrases, and with words that rhymed. A little friend nearby noticed and said, "I can sing it too." And they sang for each other taking turns page by page until the book was finished. "Let's do it again," one of them said as I moved away to observe other children around the room at play with music. (Littleton, 1998)

PRIMARY SOURCE: THE PILLSBURY STUDIES

Watching and listening to these three-year-old children play freely with music, it was obvious that self-initiated experiences were meaningful to them. Their responses contributed to my understanding of the broader issue of children's musical development and commitment to provide time for free play at the end of each music session throughout the year. Playback and analysis of the videotapes prompted more questions about how young children play with music and if freedom to play influenced their music behaviors and development. Having been enlightened by these three-year-olds about the necessity of devising more mindful approaches, open-ended strategies, and freer music activities, I decided to determine the difference in how they played with music (child directed) and how they were taught music (adult directed).

The primary impetus for further investigations came from interest in studies of young children's play with music conducted over seventy-five years ago at a school in Santa Barbara, California, established by the Pillsbury Foundation for the Advancement of Music Education. Known as the Pillsbury Studies, the stated purpose was "to undertake a study of the music of young children, to discover their natural forms of musical expression and to determine means of developing their musical capacities, particularly in the field of spontaneous creation" (Moorhead and Pond, 1941, p. 7). The music researchers, Gladys Moorhead and Donald Pond, observed and documented children's free play with music in a music-specific environment. This is the backstory of how it all began in the words of cofounder Donald Pond, taken from his 1980 article "The Young Child's Playful World of Sound":

> In 1936, attorney Evan S. Pillsbury left a legacy to establish a foundation for the advancement of music education. To determine how the funds might be most usefully spent, the three appointed trustees sought the advice of conductor Leopold Stokowski. He told them that what he thought was most needed was an in-depth study of the spon-

taneous music and musicality of young children, and he suggested that they establish a school for this purpose. Stokowski who was acquainted with my work at the Dalton School in New York City, attended by one of his daughters, recommended me for the position of the school's music director. I held that position from January 1937 to the end of December 1944. (p. 38)

From 1937 to 1948, the Pillsbury Foundation school included children ages 2 to 8 years. Gladys Moorhead and Donald Pond, in their roles as directors-facilitators-researchers kept detailed written records, including case studies of children's music making. In addition to on-site observations, they collected data on audiotape recordings of children's music making. Moorhead and Pond published four separate reports, *Music of Young Children: Introduction and Chant* (1941), *General Observations* (1942), *Musical Notation* (1944), and *Free Use of Instruments for Musical Growth* (1951). Moorhead and Pond authored the first three reports and Moorhead with Florence Sandvik and Don Wight authored the final report in 1951.

These are summaries of each report (Littleton, 1991):

I. *Music of Young Children: Introduction and Chant* (1941) documents 150 children's vocal chants that were recorded by manuscript and phonograph over a three-year period. Each chant was analyzed according to musical characteristics of rhythm and melody, social factors, physical activity, rhythmic use of materials, dramatic play, individual and group initiation, and content of verbal forms. Twenty-five representative examples of children's vocal chants were printed in musical notation and retained on phonograph recordings.

II. *General Observations* (1942) describes musical behaviors of children as individuals and in groups. These were recorded each day by diary notes. Notation and audio recording of the song content recorded all music created by the children. Moorhead and Pond observed that the songs adults teach children to sing are "in all ways unlike their own music." Music-play behaviors with instruments were classified sequentially as (1) sound exploration, and (2) rhythmic order, characteristic of "rhythmic germs" (motives). They reported that dramatic play with instruments "comes first by way of (physical) movement." Vocal dramatic play was exhibited when the child sang using specific rhythms and melodies as characterizations in an improvised music story.

III. *Musical Notation* (1944) presents an experiment in teaching musical notation over five months to one group of five- and six-year-old children who demonstrated an interest in learning to read and write music. The researchers reported conclusively that music reading and writing skills can be taught to young children and that

they are able to gain a greater understanding of rhythmic and melodic construction and acquire the perception of absolute pitch.
However, Moorhead and Pond issued several caveats concerning
the introduction of musical notation to young children: (a) children
must be instructed according to their individual maturity level; (b)
they must have had ample opportunity previously for uninhibited,
creative experiences with sound exploration; (c) they must have
gained sufficient musical experience to desire a richer musical experience; (d) they must be presented skills compatible with their
mental and emotional growth; and (e) technical studies (musical
symbolization) should be related to the child's instinct for creativity, and adapted to stimulate creative activity. Furthermore, they
reaffirmed their philosophical position on children's music making: "For us music is primarily creative and only secondarily inter-
pretative; that for us the child's deepest necessity, to which all
other things must be made subservient, is not that he may be able
to read and to interpret other composers' music but that he may be
able to write his own" (p. 79).

IV. *Free Use of Instruments for Musical Growth* (1951) describes how
children develop musically through free use of instruments. Case
studies were conducted with three boys approximately four to five
years old who were selected for their individual differences and
interests. Carl demonstrated interest in tone production with instruments. Roy exhibited through drumming the relationship between physical movement and sound production and, later, rhythmic patterning. Jay, who had been in the school a year longer than
the other two, demonstrated more varied musical experience
through rhythmic, tonal, and formal patterns, and the ability to
express musical ideas on instruments. Daily diary notations of musical characteristics, selection of instruments, and individual and
group play were recorded for each boy for six months, three
months, and seven months, respectively. The researchers summarized that each child explored instruments differently and "produced music that was recognizably different from other children"
(Moorhead and Pond, 1941, p. 116). These children were interested
in and learned from the instrument playing of other children. From
their observations and analysis, Moorhead and Pond concluded
"free use of varied instruments led to growth in understanding
timbre, pitch, vibration, rhythm, tonal relationships and melody.
The children showed increasing power to express their ideas and
feelings in spontaneous music and to develop musical communication with one another" (p. 117).

MUSIC SETTING, INSTRUMENTS, AND MATERIALS

Preparation of the free-play environment and selection of musical instruments were essential to the rationale and objectives of the studies. The musical environment was designed to emphasize children's freedom to make music and develop social understanding and responsibility, "which would give them power to maintain their own activities and organizations with the minimum of adult intervention" (1941). The founders believed that for young children to explore and create music of their own, apart from the music adults taught them, they required a musically rich and inviting place that included other children with whom they could play. In such a setting, adults were present to offer assistance and provide information, if invited. Similarly, the adult role included safety supervision and transitions, as needed.

Deliberations concerned the selection of musical instruments focused on: musical quality, a variety of tone colors, whether instruments were technically suited for use by young children, and if they were freely available and portable. Instruments and sound-making materials were chosen in the interest and delight of children for optimum motivation and opportunity to play, experiment, and explore.

The Pillsbury Foundation school attracted benefactors who wished to loan or donate musical instruments. Mr. Henry Eichheim offered Asian instruments from his collection: *sarons* from Bali and Java, Chinese gongs, Burmese gongs, a variety of bells in various shapes and sizes from China, Chinese cymbals, drums from India, a double-headed tom-tom from Korea, a single-headed Japanese theater drum, and a Chinese theater drum. Mrs. Frederic S. Gould provided a large bronze Japanese gong. Over time, the school added flute-like recorders, a 2.5-octave marimba, other gongs, finger cymbals, maracas, a set of temple blocks, and guitar. Musical equipment included a recording unit, phonograph player, and comprehensive library of recordings including music from plainsong to twentieth-century composers and folk music of twenty-eight different countries from Europe, America, Africa, and Asia.

The Pillsbury Studies were unprecedented in their design and constituent elements:

- Moorhead and Pond based their studies on the premise that to understand children's music making, you must learn it from them.
- They were the first to conduct comprehensive investigations of children's spontaneous music behaviors in the context of free play.
- All studies were conducted in the children's natural habitat, at a time set aside.
- Musical materials and instruments were attractive, familiar, safe, and always available.
- True-to-life data were gathered by observations in real time.

- The studies were conducted over ten years according to the same goals and in the same setting.

Why then were these successful results ignored for so many years? Primarily, it was the rapid educational change in the following era that shifted attention away from the social emphasis on human development to increased interest in the scientific pursuits of cognition. The prominence in and preference for quantification rendered the descriptive, anecdotal observations and analyses of the Pillsbury Studies' findings insignificant and irrelevant. However, with a view to more recent findings by ecological psychologists and play researchers, today the Pillsbury Studies provide a rich source for the study of children's music-making behaviors in music-specific play environments, when music instruments as play materials are available, with the presence of peers and absence of adult intervention. Overall, these studies provide a view of children as they experience opportunities to play freely without restraint in a noninstructional setting.

THEORIES OF CHILDREN'S PLAY

All but forgotten, the father of the kindergarten, Friedrich Wilhelm August Fröebel (1782–1852), a student of Johann Heinrich Pestalozzi (1746–1872), placed the importance of play at the center of children's development. For more than two hundred years, powerful voices from philosophy, psychology, pedagogy, and advanced systems of thought have agreed that play prevails as the primary factor in young children's learning.

Children's free play has been investigated from numerous perspectives. Mildred Parten (1932, 1933) pioneered the study of social play among preschool children. Charlotte Bühler (1935) and Karl Bühler (1930) investigated young children's cognitive play development before Jean Piaget. Each of these studies were prototypes that influenced future play research: Piaget's (1962) cognitive theory of children's play, and Sara Smilansky's (1968) modification of Piaget's play stages and her studies of social-dramatic play. Russian psychologist Lev Vygotsky's work on play was imbedded in his conception of mental-social-cultural elements of child development (1978). Unfortunately, politics and an early death at thirty-seven silenced his powerful voice. Yet Vygotsky's work became widely recognized and respected during the late 1970s, and it continues to be so in the present. Considerable interest in Vygotsky's and Piaget's theories advanced the scholarship on child development. Comparisons of their work resulted in discussion and dispute.

In 1962 Piaget wrote a touching statement of regret concerning Vygotsky and his work:

It is not without sadness that an author discovers, twenty-five years after its publication, the work of a colleague who has died in the meantime, when that work contains so many points of immediate interest to him which should have been discussed personally and in detail. Although my friend A. Luria kept me up-to-date concerning Vygotsky's sympathetic and yet critical position with respect to my work, I was never able to read his writings or to meet him in person, and in reading his book today, I regret this profoundly, for we could have come to an understanding on a number of points. (www.marxists.org/archive/vygotsky/works/comment/piaget.htm)[4]

CULTURAL PERSPECTIVES OF PLAY

Johan Huizinga (1872–1945), Dutch cultural historian and theorist, proposed an expansive and innovative theory of play, culture, and human development. His classic work *Homo Ludens: The Study of the Play-Element in Human Culture* (1938, translated in 1944–1950) continues as the prevailing influence on any serious scholar concerning play theory. Huizinga conceptualized "man the player" (the playing human) across civilizations from the mighty Greeks to the modern age. Across a wide intellectual swath, Huizinga presented the concept of play as a civilizing force expressed in language and law, philosophy and art, and even war. Roger Callois (1913–1978), French social theorist, recognized Huizinga's "original and powerful work," *Homo Ludens.* Callois wrote:

> This work, although most of its premises are debatable, is nonetheless capable of opening extremely fruitful avenues to research and reflection. In any case, it is permanently to J. Huizinga's credit that he has masterfully analyzed several of the fundamental characteristics of play and has demonstrated the importance of its role in the very development of civilization. (p. 3)

Perhaps too much scholarship has focused on conflicts in thought between Huizinga and Callois. Although they overlapped in time, the two men were a generation apart.[5] Callois's perspective in *Man, Play and Games* (translated in 1961) concerned the explication of game theory. He examined global and culturally specific games as functions of socialization. He categorized games as play forms: *agon* (sports and contests of skills and chance), *alea* (casinos, racetracks, lotteries), *mimicry* (puppet shows, carnivals, masked balls), and *ilinx* (traveling shows and annual occasions for merrymaking and jollity).

Brian Sutton-Smith, in *The Ambiguity of Play* (1997), analyzed play theory from anthropology, biology, psychology, and sociology, all fields within his considerable expertise. His extensive research, vast knowledge, and superb scholarship contributed authenticity, raised the level of inquiry in play studies, and advanced the quality of future investigations.

His work guided all who would pursue studies on play in human culture and development. Sutton-Smith loved stories, his own, those of others, particularly children's. Early in his career, he collected folklore from his native New Zealand. Through stories and games, he discovered the irresistible phenomena of play. Always mindful of the child's perspective, Sutton-Smith used narrative, discourse, and empirical research to establish a preeminent voice in the scholarship of play theory. With characteristic jest, he called himself "a young Marco Polo of play."

AESTHETIC PERSPECTIVES OF PLAY

Enlightenment ideas of the late seventeenth and eighteenth centuries embraced the romance of imagination. It was a time of social, political, and artistic change for individual freedom, openly expressive arts, and the idealization of the innocent child. A list of who's who includes thinkers, poets, musicians, artists, and rulers who sailed atop the crest of this new wave of humanism: Rousseau, Voltaire, Kant, Goethe, Mozart, Delacroix, Hapsburg emperor Joseph II, Frederick the Great of Prussia, and Catherine the Great of Russia. Play and art, once the sole purview of high culture, now extended to and captured the imagination of popular culture.

Following the ideas of Immanuel Kant (1724–1804), Friedrich Schiller (1795–1845), in *On the Aesthetic Education of Man in a Series of Letters* put forth a theory of art that linked beauty and play as elements of the same domain. He asserted that the value of play is play for play's sake, for delight, pleasure, and absent of necessity or extrinsic reward. Schiller's most important contribution to play theory was the introduction of play categories: (a) material superfluity, resulting in physical play, and (b) aesthetic superfluity, emerging as aesthetic or dramatic play. A century later Herbert Spencer (1820–1903) in *The Principles of Psychology* extended Schiller's assertion that aesthetic sentiments originated from the play impulse. According to Sutton-Smith, "He [Schiller] is the first influential social scientist in the Anglo-American tradition to consider child play and child art to be for scientific study" (1997, p. 133).

HISTORICAL PERSPECTIVES OF PLAY

Huizinga, in his classic text *Homo Ludens*, declared that humans in their earliest stages played; and that the play-spirit of joy, pretend, and nonseriousness has been a major civilizing force in human development:

> Ritual grew up in sacred play, poetry was born and nourished on play, [and that] and music and dancing were pure play. Wisdom and philosophy found expressions in words and forms derived from religious

contests. The rules of warfare, the conventions of noble living were built on play patterns. We have to conclude, therefore, that civilization is, in its earliest phases, played. (p. 173)

. . . Mediaeval life was brimful of play: the joyous and unbuttoned play of the people, full of pagan elements that had lost their sacred significance and been transformed into jesting and buffoonery, or the solemn and pompous play of chivalry, the sophisticated play of courtly love. (p. 179)

Huizinga asserted that throughout history, play and music were bonded by values that transcended logic, the visible, and the tangible; and that the primary quality of play is aesthetic. Huizinga said that the play-element reached its full flower in the eighteenth century. He attributed this conclusion to the supreme importance of eighteenth-century music, and its perfect balance of play content and aesthetic content. Unequivocally, he proclaimed, "Music is the highest and purest expression of the *facultas ludendi*" (p. 187).

A GENIUS AT PLAY

In a word, Mozart! Could he have been Mozart in any other era? A true embodiment of the play-spirit, his was no ordinary life. From childhood excitement of touring Europe and England like a rock star to adult disappointment and challenges of loss, poverty, and poor health, Mozart retained his youthful exuberance for life, love, pleasure, and fancy clothes. Ever optimistic, egocentric, and hyperactive, his genius flourished until the end. Mozart lived life as play; he composed that way too. This is how he described his composing process in a personal letter to Baron V. in response to his questions on the topic:

I now come to the most difficult part of your letter, which I would willingly pass over in silence, for here my pen denies me at its service. Still I will try, even at the risk of being well laughed at. You say, you should like to know my way of composing, and what method I follow in writing works of some extent. I can really say no more on the subject than the following for I myself know no more about it, and cannot account for it. When I am, as it were, completely myself, entirely alone, and of good cheer say, travelling in a carriage, or walking after a good meal, or during the night when I cannot sleep; it is on such occasions that my ideas flow best and most abundantly. Whence and how they come, I know not; nor can I force them. Those ideas that please me I retain in memory, and am accustomed, as I have been told, to hum them to myself. If I continue in this way, it soon occurs to me how I may turn this or that morsel to account, so as to make a good dish of it, that is to say, agreeably to the rules of counterpoint, to the peculiarities of various instruments, etc.

ly than language and is more difficult; instead, we argue that music learning matches the speed and effort of language acquisition. We conclude that music merits a central place in our understanding of human development. (p. 1)

MOTHER-INFANT MUSIC PLAY

Descriptive studies conducted with children birth to age five in natural settings provide additional perspectives on how young children engage with music. In 1998 I conducted a series of mother-infant studies of music-play interactions; specifically, vocalizations, rhythmic physical movement, and actions with sound-making toys. Home visits were made to observe music interactions between mothers and their infants from three to ten months old. On separate occasions, each mother was interviewed and completed a survey. From interviews, surveys, transcription, and playback analyses of videotaped sessions, it was concluded that:

1. When mothers exhibited musical behaviors by singing, vocalizing, chanting, moving rhythmically, producing rhythmic patterns with toys, singing with recorded music, moving in response to music, their infants responded by turning toward the sound, establishing eye contact, showing facial animation, and demonstrating increasing physical movement, vocalizing, and sound-making actions with toys.
2. When infants exhibited eye contact, sustained gaze, smiles, changes in facial expressions, reflexive physical movements, intentional physical movements, cooing, squealing, and tonal vocalizations, mothers responded by attempting to imitate precisely their infant's music behaviors, attempting to sustain their infant's attention to music behaviors, and attempting to maintain the infant's music-play actions.
3. When infants initiated a new music-play action, mothers responded by prompting face-to-face eye contact, displaying positive facial expressions, exploring variations in vocal pitch, dynamics, and tempo, introducing sound-making toys, altering their infant's physical position, adjusting amount of tactile contact, and adjusting the amount of physical stimulation.
4. Developmental differences were observed in infants' music-play behaviors: (a) All displayed interest in music play; (b) all are capable of deliberate vocal behaviors, of intentional physical movements in response to music, and of goal-oriented actions with sound-making toys; (c) younger infants display less fine and gross motor skills than older infants; however, younger infants are capable of a wide range of vocal pitch, timbre, and dynamics; (d) infants use their voices to initiate, facilitate, and sustain music play

interactions with their mothers; (e) older infants demonstrate greater diversity in movement responses and in play with sound-making toys.[18]

Scientific evidence confirms human infants are born wired for music. What does this mean for music educators engaged in pedagogy and research? First, we must consider whether music training and instruction are needed or advised for the very young. Further, we need to know about children's innate musicality before we prescribe adult-directed instruction. Vignettes of young children's play with music are necessary to supplement empirical findings. Descriptive studies offer ethnographic realism and contribute to a wider-canvas view of children's musicality and its development. Seeking that wider view, a series of qualitative studies were conducted to understand how young children play freely with music (Littleton, 1991, 1992, 1994, 1997, 1998, and 2002). Studies of free-play behaviors of twenty-two four-year-old children were set in a prepared music playroom to understand how children might make music without teacher direction or intervention.[19] My study focused on three established play categories: cognitive, according to Piaget and Smilansky; social, following Parten's work; and musical, identified by the Pillsbury Studies. Each of these categories was divided into three subsets. The cognitive category was defined as functional play (exploring, seeking, imitating), constructive play (building, making, producing) and dramatic play (imagining, role-playing, fantasizing). Social play included playing alone (solitary play), playing independently but aware of others (parallel play), and playing cooperatively with others (group play). The music-play category was divided by vocal music behaviors (vocalizing rhythmically, singing, chanting), instrumental music behaviors (playing and manipulating musical instruments and sound sources other than musical instruments), and moving to music (responding to music of one's own making or that of others' vocalizations and instrument playing). The following excerpts, transcribed from videotapes of selected cognitive, social, and music-play episodes, demonstrate young children's free play in a music setting.[20]

CHILDREN'S COGNITIVE MUSIC-PLAY BEHAVIORS

Exploring sounds and seeking techniques of eliciting sounds with musical instruments characterize functional play of young children. The following episode describes the four-year-old children's first playdate in the music setting.[21]

The children enter the music room quietly. No one talks. They wander around the room as each one chooses instruments and music-play materials. There is no discussion or negotiations about choices of play materials. Caroline begins to play with the Chinese gong, softly, randomly, exploring its sounds. Lori picks up the violin, struggles with the bow as she slowly, quietly draws it across the strings. Two boys begin to play with the xylophones. Another begins to explore the electronic keyboard. The activity and level of sound gradually increase as more children begin to play. The resulting sounds are either rhythmic and patterned within a steady pulse or nonmetric and random. Whether brief or extended, the children's explorations appear intentional, self-initiated, and independently created.

Functional play is serious and invites opportunities for sustained interest. One little girl discovered the violin and played with it exclusively:

A playmate asked her friend, "Tara, why don't you play some music?" Tara tries the violin. It squeaks, and both girls laugh. Tara experiments with different ways of holding the violin and bow. She concentrates carefully on drawing the bow across open strings. She experiments with faster/slower movements of the bow, but makes no effort to produce any discernible rhythmic or melodic patterns; instead she is focuses on the sound quality. Clearly, she dislikes the scratchy, squeaky sounds she first made. Patiently, she seeks to make improvements by adjusting her holding and bowing techniques. She explains to her playmate, "I've never played the violin before. I have to practice." At the end of the session, Tara runs to meet her mother, who was there to take her home, and shows her how she can play the violin. In a session the next day, Tara picks up the violin again and plays for an extended period of time.

Holly complains: "Don't play that violin. It's squeaky!"

Tara: "It isn't squeaky. I've tested it. Here let me show you this thing." (She takes rosin from the violin case and rubs it on the bow.) "This is fun!"

Holly: " I KNOW! I have a violin at home."

Tara: "Do you take lessons?"

Holly: "NO!"

Tara: "I want to take lessons."

Holly: "I've played "Jingle Bells" on my violin before."

Tara: "Well, I've never seen a violin before, so I need to play it."

In a later session, Tara shows continued interest in violin playing and shares her enthusiasm with another playmate:

Jenny: (Struggles with holding and playing the violin at the same time.) "Today, it's [the violin] not so good! I've gotta get this medicine in it." (She takes the rosin and administers it to the bow.)

Tara: "What happened to it?"

Jenny: "It's not really broken. I'm pretending. OK?"

Tara: (worried) "How's it broken?"

Jenny: (irritated) "I'M KIDDING!"

Tara: (worried) "How's it broken, though?"

Jenny: "See . . . everybody keeps testing it (violin) . . . and it got so old . . . and, uh . . . beat up. (She changes her natural speaking voice to a pretend voice.) "It's ok. Now, you can use it. I washed it off. I went to the violin store and they polished it."

Tara: "FOR REAL?"

Jenny: "NO! FOR PLAY!"

Jenny leaves the violin with Tara and goes across the room to play the piano. Tara takes the violin again and draws the bow across open strings. She discovers a convenient and comfortable way to hold and play the instrument at the same time. She sits on the floor with the base of the violin resting on the floor and the scroll leaning against her chest, similar to a cello player. She manages one hand for holding the violin and the other to bow it. She is pleased.

In his first play session, Daniel explored several instruments, one at a time. A week later, he revisited many of the same instruments with new ideas.

Daniel chooses cymbals and plays briefly. He puts them down and picks up the violin. He has difficulty holding it with one hand and bowing with the other. He tries to place the violin under his chin with the wrong end (scroll) and cannot support it. Jenny sees him and says, "I'll show you how that goes, honey." She takes the violin and places it correctly under his chin. He plays for less than a minute and moves on to a tom-tom drum nearby. He selects two xylophone mallets and uses them to play the drum. He says, "Man, this is going to play music!" He explores several rhythm patterns . . . slowly. Later in the session, Daniel played the tom-tom and an African drum at the same time with one hand on each. He improvises a singing chant as he plays the drums. Next, he adds the cymbals interspersed between the playing of the drums. He does an American Indian dance while playing the African drum. He picks up the violin and sings a made-up song and walks around the room. He gives the violin to Jenny, goes to the Chinese gong and plays it louder and louder until it falls over. He leaves it and finds the bongo drums, returns to the gong, plays both instruments, and sings.

The distinction between functional play behaviors and constructive play behaviors may seem difficult to differentiate. To explain, children's functional play with music is best described as free exploration, vocally and/or with instruments and movement. Constructive play is character-ized by children's music making that exhibits intentional, discernible rhythmic patterns, melodic patterns, tempo, dynamics, and timbre within a recognizable form or structure. The following episode demonstrates a remarkable example of making and producing musical ideas and struc-tures.

In the first music-play session, Caroline chooses the Chinese gong and begins to strike it with the mallet provided. Her movements are repetitive and quick as she listens to the sounds. Pausing, she looks around the room. Soon, she begins to repeat a pattern of eight to ten beats, from slower to faster, softer to louder. Without a break in concentration, she repeats the same pattern fifteen times in succession. She pauses and re-peats the exact same pattern seven more times. The gong-playing episode continues uninterrupted for twenty minutes.

Caroline's improvised music with the gong exhibited purposeful, or-ganized elements of tempo, dynamics, rhythm, duration, and expressive phrasing within an audible structure. Each repetition was identical. A week later when Caroline returned to the music setting, she went directly to the gong and began to play the *exact same music* she played before. Her musical creation had remained in her memory long after play was over. She returned to the gong several times during the eight-week play ses-sions and each time played her signature opus. She called it "The Ancient Hitter."

Caroline's play was constructive and solitary. The following is an ex-ample of constructive and cooperative play when two boys created a musical event I call Dueling Xylophones.

Greg and Ken engage in a musical game of their own making with the contrabass xylophone bars. Each boy has a set of mallets and takes turns playing the three tone bars tuned to C, E, G. After a few turns, they begin to imitate each other's playing in a dueling performance. Soon they add leaps, jumps, and exaggerated arm movements to the musical phrases they create. They do not speak to each other. They communicate in a musical conversation within a steady beat of rhythms, melodic patterns, tempo, dynamics, and duration, each copying from the other or raising the challenge level with new ideas.

The boys recreated variations on C-E-G many times during the next few weeks. Each boy found other boys and girls as willing partners for Dueling Xylophones. Children simultaneously danced and sang as they

played. Another interesting episode involved Holly and Tara; they created the Tambourine Dance.

Each girl with a tambourine improvises a dance of jumps, turns, and
sways. They take turns—without speaking—and copy each other's improvised, rhythmic dance with tambourine. As the dances continue, they
explore different ways to move and play, all the while giggling with
delight and satisfaction. A new idea is introduced, dancing with tambourines on their heads. With their hands free, they pick up small drums and
bells and play them while dancing and shaking their tambourine heads.
They continue raising the levels of complexity and challenge like a couple
of jazz players—until time runs out.

In a distinctive vocal example of solitary, constructive play, Belinda
improvises a lengthy song in rhyme, suggesting the form and style of the
blues. She holds the violin like a guitar and strums as she sings:

> I woke up this morning and—there's no way
> I said I went to bed and—no pay
> I came up—but I didn't know what to say
> La-la-la-la-la
>
> I told him what I should do
> I didn't know what—
> And he said—And he said
> do-Do-dooo
>
> And all the people in the world
> And he said la-La-la
> And I woke up my baby, and my baby said . . .
> Waaa-waaa-waaa

Dramatic play, the third subset of the cognitive play category, occurs
when children pretend to be somebody or something else. They imitate
other people in action and speech, often with the aid of real or imagined
objects. In the music setting, the instruments were used variously in
creating musical and nonmusical play themes.

In one dramatic play episode, Jay says, "Pretend this is my room."
This announcement sparks a flurry of group activity in building a play-
house made of music instruments. First, they outline the house with xylophone mallets placed on the floor and, next, furnish the rooms with xylophones. One by one, children bring all the remaining music instruments
into the music house. Quickly children establish their own personal
spaces. Jay negotiates: "You can't have this. This is my room. Pretend me
and Jenny have to stay in our room, because we don't know where to go,
because we are blind." The children continue cooperatively constructing
the music house until all the available instruments are brought inside.
Jenny calls out: "What about the PIANO? (Obviously too big to move.)
Oh, gosh we can leave that!" She plays very loud sounds in the lowest

register of the piano and shouts: "It's lightening! Put on the roof!" Jay shouts: "Hurry! Get into our house!" Belinda: "Oh no! It's raining!" When all the children are physically inside, Jenny says: "We are all snug and tight inside! Now, we are cuddly inside." They pass instruments to each other all the while sharing and playing together.

The next dialogue is transcribed intact and in sequence during a lengthy and remarkable example of cooperative-dramatic play. Belinda calls out, "Let's do "Jingle Bells"!" All children sing "Jingle Bells" and play metal-ringing bells, triangles, and cymbals. "This looks like a house! Look, we cleaned the whole (music) room up." Jenny introduces another new idea: "Time for bedtime!" she sings, as she rings the triangle. All lie down on the floor and pretend to sleep. Soon after, Jenny rings the triangle again and sings: "Time to get up." Several other children echo: "Thank goodness! Thank goodness!" Next, Jenny announces, "Time for breakfast," in the same way, singing and ringing the triangle. The others follow her suggestion and use the music instruments as pretend utensils and food items. Still in control, Jenny sings out: "Play—time." At this juncture, Jay introduces yet another play theme: "Pretend it was Christmas!" Belinda picks up his lead: "And Santa Claus comes to our house FIRST! Just like he always did." Jenny: "Yeah, and we say it's midnight." All the children pretend to sleep. Then, without any verbal cues, they jump up simultaneously and yell: "HE'S HERE! HE'S HERE!" They continue yelling and playing instruments: "Look what I got! Look what I got! Jenny excites the group: "Oh, my gosh. WE GOT A WHOLE PLAY-ROOM!" All yelling and cheering: "He brought us all the toys we wanted! We're rich! Look what he gave me." Belinda, still fond of the violin, says to another child: "Give me that violin! That's what Santa Claus gave me." Jenny: "I've got an instrument crown!" as she place a tambourine on her head. She suggests a novel idea: "We got to talk in French!" She chatters in a high-pitched voice, speaking and then singing in her invented French babble. Nearby, Jay joins in and tries to imitate Jenny. He interjects: "Look what Santa got me." He plays the Autoharp, his gift from Santa. The play episode ends when Jenny says: "He gave us all these toys!" and Jay concludes: "He gave us all the toys—and we SHARE!"

In another dramatic play episode, a particular instrument is used in nonmusical ways. Holly says, "Let's play dentist. I'm the dentist, ok? We need mirrors." She searches the room and finds the small brass finger cymbals. "We can use these. Come here, patient!" The play theme does not progress. No one wants to be the dental patient.

Jenny introduces a fantasy dental patient to keep the play theme going as she employs the instruments in nonmusical and unusual treatments. She uses the xylophone mallets, one in each hand, as walking canes. She pretends to be an old lady walking unsteadily while her knees wobble, her hands shake, and her voice is high-pitched and weak. Margaret asks,

"Who's that?" Jenny replies, "My grandmother. Her teeth are falling out." Margaret: "Here, Grandmother. We'll take her to the dentist. Margaret assumes the role of dentist. Jenny's the grandmother. Margaret uses a triangle striker to look inside Grandmother's mouth. She places finger cymbals and metal tone bars from the glockenspiel on Grandmother's head for treatment. Each imaginary dental tool was selected from a shiny metal musical instrument or part of one. The mention that Grandmother needed medicine sent Margaret to the violin case for rosin (the designated medicine from an earlier episode). Jenny said, "Every twenty-five minutes I have to take it."

In the roles of superheroes, boys made creative and unusual use of the instruments. Jay announces, "I'm the big turtle!" He waves two metal triangle strikers around as weapons. Ryan joins the play with the claves as they engage in a mock sword fight. They make vocal sound effects as they leap about thrusting the weapons at each other in a ninja-warrior game. They are careful and do not touch each other or make any contact with the weapons. Jay shouts, "Cowabunga!" Ryan echoes, "Cowabunga!" Jay adds, "Hey, dude. Let's get a pizza." They use the tall African drums with shoulder straps as their weapons carrier. They place triangle strikers, claves, finger cymbals and other small music instruments inside their weapons-carrier-drum as they interject: "Here's mine!" "This one's mine!" "Who's gonna be Raphael?" "I'm Leonardo!" . . . "OK, space-man."

Many dramatic role-playing themes in the music setting involve kings, queens, and princesses, members of a family, Disney characters, and a music teacher/conductor, the latter a favored role of authority. Margaret, the first to assume the music teacher role, sets the example for all who come after her. She organizes and directs all the children to be her students. First, she assigns an instrument to each one, demonstrates where each should sit, and gives instructions when to play. Margaret maintained remarkable control of her students for the duration of the thirty-minute music lesson.

With students in place, Margaret takes the central position behind the music stand and raises her conductor's baton. "When I go like that . . ." She strikes the music stand with the baton. "That means stop" (playing the instruments). "Wait! Wait! . . . Go, Jenny! Go, Amy! Go, Jay! Go, Belinda!" Each child responds by playing their instrument as Margaret shouts, "Go!" She explains that when she yells, "Switch!" the children must quickly run to a different instrument. Margaret continues rhythmically calling out student's names as they begin to play their second instrument assignment. Realizing her students need more guidance, she leaves her position behind the music stand and goes to each student indicating exactly when he or she should commence playing. She waits until each one begins to play according to her instruction before moving to the next student. Some students ignore her and play outside the conductor/music teacher's established rules. Margaret immediately returns to the music stand to give more orders. "I've already said this once! You need to move on a little bit. Okay? Switch! No, no. You come here." She leads the student by the arm. Growing tired of this, the group begins to challenge Margaret's directives. The complaints get louder and louder until she takes firm control. "SHHHHHHH! SHHHHHHH!" They stop talking and listen to her. She continues directing individual students:

> Go. Go. Go. Go. No. I didn't say "go" to you. Now, Amy stopped at the right time. When I went like that [she taps the baton on the music stand] she stopped. Amy stopped at the right time.

Margaret uses various behavior-control techniques, including praise, tapping students on their heads, leading them by the arm, striking the music stand with the baton, and giving verbal commands. She insists students move at the proper time in the sequence she established at the beginning of her lesson/rehearsal. Margaret commands: "Raise your hand if you've stopped [playing]."[22] Everyone obeys and the room is momentarily totally silent. Play resumes and continues until Jenny says, "I wanna be the teacher now." Margaret thinks of a quick reply to maintain her position, placate Jenny, and discourage any other challenger. Speaking to Jenny: "You are a teacher. You are my daughter." Pointing to other children, she says, "You two are my helpers, and you and you and you are my helpers." Like Toscanini, she maintains firm control.

In a solitary-constructive play episode, Holly created a one-girl band with a variety of musical instruments. She sits on a drum as she plays soft-to-loud sequences on the gong. Abruptly, she jumps up and runs to get the Autoharp and attempts to place it on her lap, but she cannot hold it and play at the same time. She solves the problem by placing the instrument on the piano bench so she can strum it with a triangle striker. Suddenly, she has a new idea. She brings the drum and a mallet over to the piano bench. With the drum placed on the floor and Autoharp on the piano bench, she plays both instruments. Holly invents a clever way to make sounds on both instruments resonate together. First, she strums the Autoharp strings with the striker in one hand and presses down one of the chord keys with the other. Adroitly, she drops the striker, picks up the mallet and plays the drum as the strings continue to resonate. This four-year-old makes her own unique music as she uses the sounds of resonating strings and reverberating percussion. She turns her attention solely to the Autoharp and experiments by simultaneously striking the strings, pressing and releasing the chord bar, and listening to the sounds. Randomly, she selects different chords and continues strumming while pressing the chord buttons. It is obvious that certain chords are especially pleasing, because she plays them over and over.

CHILDREN'S SOCIAL MUSIC-PLAY BEHAVIORS

Throughout the study, the children played together more frequently than they played alone. Group play is based on children's communication and cooperation. Play continues or disperses according to the players' interest in the play theme, their willingness to accept its limitations, and ability to sustain play. Children's parallel play differs from cooperative group play by the absence of direct communication. As children in the present study played instruments independently, they often imitated the music of other players from across the room or nearby. For example, Greg's and Ken's spontaneous improvisations with the contrabass xylophone bars were picked up by Meghan. Already playing the soprano xylophone on her own, when the boys began playing, she copied their rhythm patterns on her instrument. The boys did not notice her or her playing and neither did she show any awareness of them, only the rhythms they played. Similar incidences occurred in another episode when Greg improvised what he called "The Haunted House," which he played on the electronic keyboard. Nearby, Sam found the violin and added an accompaniment to Greg's improvisation. He imitated Greg's musical tempo, dynamics, and haunted house expressions—all without conversation, collaboration, or acknowledgment from Greg. Another parallel play event involved note-by-note imitation. The music playroom was equipped with several melodic percussion instruments, xylophones, metallophones, glockenspiels, contrabass xylophone tone bars, a piano, and electronic keyboard. As Amy played the first three phrases of "Hot Cross Buns" on a bass xylophone, nearby, Meghan played the same tune on a soprano xylophone. Neither girl spoke or acknowledged the other's presence. Nevertheless, it was obvious by what they played that they made music together.

In summary, these vignettes demonstrate the importance of socialization and its function in the music-play culture of young children; and conversely they demonstrate the importance of the music-play culture in fostering high-functioning social interactions. Frequently, children instructed each other concerning how to play an instrument or how to create music together by playing several instruments in a spontaneous musical ensemble of their own making. Consistently and over time, they listened to and imitated others' music making. In several episodes, they took turns assuming the role of music teacher by directing others in well-organized lessons, rehearsals, and concert activities. Furthermore, they joined together in creating extended music dramas complete with *leitmotifs* (recurring music themes). The musical ideas, spontaneous compositions, and mini-operas produced by these children were in all ways different from the standard music content and practices that emphasize music learning by rote or note. Specifically, when children were left alone to make music: (1) They showed increasing understanding of the expressive power of rhythm and tempo, tone colors and dynamics, and melodic and tonal characteristics; (2) they demonstrated the ability to develop musical communication with each other in the creation of imaginative, structured, and sensitive vocal and instrumental compositions.

In all ways that matter, this study gives evidence that music made by children for children in the child's world is in part defined by the exclusivity of their shared experience and common knowledge. In other words, given an opportunity to play freely with music, children and adults do not exhibit similar behaviors. Adults who are not trained musicians are more likely to disregard an opportunity to play with instruments, or they dabble a bit and quit.[23] I believe that free play with music offers the young child unique opportunities to create a temporary world compatible with his or her musical abilities, interests, desires, and needs—a world apart from the music culture of adults.

PEDAGOGY AND PLAY

These studies initiated from a strong desire to know what children *already* knew and enjoyed about music. How might we communicate musically with children without direct instruction? Given the vast body of literature on the developmental and educational importance of children's play, why have so few inquiries involved music? My studies of children's play in music-specific settings conducted over several years yielded important findings and generated new insights concerning music learning and teaching. Few applications and replications of these studies have been reported, in part because teachers are concerned about the practicallity of letting children freely play with music. Assumptions include incorrect beliefs that play creates a permissive atmosphere, makes too much noise, results in damage to instruments, and takes time away from real learning.

First, one must accept the premise that playing *is* learning, not antithetical to learning. Then one must agree that playful learning enriches children's experience of music. Additionally, one must understand that planning for play-centered activities requires as much attention to musical and behavioral goals, acquiring materials, and applying procedures as important as any other means of instruction. Additionally, strategies concerning play must be thoughtfully incorporated into one's teaching routine so that teacher and children know what to expect. Successfully incorporating new ideas, approaches, and methods concerning play takes time and practice (*what* to teach) supported by philosophical foundations (*why* teach). This holds true for studying and applying principles and practices according to Carl Orff, Zoltán Kodály, Emile Jacques-Dalcroze, or Shinichi Suzuki.

Each manifestation of play offers a broad and diverse range of experiences, teacher-directed play, teacher-guided play, and child-directed play. There is no "stage theory" applicable here, no sequence of concepts, or linear development of skills. Instead, the nature of play is distinguished by major themes of this book, children's individualization, imagination, and invention. Through a process that is fluid, boundless, and transcendent, play creates a *portage* between what is known in the present to the discovery of new knowledge. Children need not be taught to play, for them play is intrinsic, biological, and driven by their need to know and learn. Play is the child's tool for learning; therefore, play and academic learning are not incompatible.

Teachers who wish to provide playful learning experiences have available a continuum of options: teacher as director of play experiences, teacher as a guide to play opportunities, teacher as a coplayer, and teacher as a nonparticipating observer. Teachers who have a playful attitude, an affinity for improvisation, and willingness to let children lead, are sure to make new discoveries about their students' musical understanding, skills, and interests as they engage playfully.

RIGGING THE PLAY ENVIRONMENT

Integrating play experiences with music might be compared to planning learning centers. Consider the children you teach, the settings and spaces available, music-teaching materials, the time allotted, and the boundaries and structure needed for a successful experience. Caution: Too much intervention and too many restrictions result in a teacher-directed lesson. When adults take over, free play stops.

- In what settings do you teach formal, structured, fixed music schedule, or less formal, open classroom, with flexible time for music? Do you teach infant, toddler, and/or threes and fours in private music classes with or without parent participation? Do you teach children in an after-care setting? Do you teach private music lessons for individual children or small groups?
- Who are the children you teach, what are their ages, how many are enrolled in a given class? Are there children with special needs?
- What musical instruments, equipment, and teaching materials are available to you? Are there ample supplies for the number of children you teach?
- Is the space in which you teach inadequate, adequate, or exceptional for your music lessons? What, if any, adjustments to the space are needed?

As you ponder these questions, consider whether the following play activities might be applicable to your teaching style and environment:

At the end of music circle-time with very young children or a music lesson with elementary school children, set aside ten or fifteen minutes for children to play. You may wish to guide children's attention to musical ideas from your lesson and invite them to make play choices from the instruments, books, pictures, or other materials you introduce. Depending on the final activity, rather than formally ending the lesson, offer a gradual and unhurried transition from teacher-directed, to teacher-guided, or free-play activities.

Within a teacher-directed lesson, allow time for brief, free explorations with instruments, movement, or singing appropriate to the children's interests and maturity. Invite children to extend, explore, or improvise in response to music inspired by the lesson. The sight of a video camera stimulates most children's interest and willingness to sing, dance, and play instruments of their own making.

Children like to see themselves and others perform. On the last day of school, my graduating fifth grade viewed videos of their kindergarten impromptu music performances. Even at that tender age, they "couldn't believe we were that small." As the laughter died down, they sang and played along with their younger selves.

Create a music play space where you can set up a video camera so children can make their own music videos. Performing for the camera excites their imagination for spontaneous singing and for singing favorite songs together with dancing and playing instruments. Some children like to use props and outfits to embellish their own performances or those of music stars. Rarely did children lip-sync to recorded music, they preferred to sing accompanied by the instrumental track.

Several teachers who explored these and their own play strategies reported that simply observing and/or conducting informal studies gave them new teaching ideas and increased their understanding of children's musicality. Successfully incorporating free-play music experiences with children in preschool and kindergarten through grade five relies on several factors: (1) carefully planned play environments for music, including (2) ample space, time, and materials for music making; (3) guidelines clearly communicated, appropriate for the children involved, and with suitable limits on behavior; (4) adult supervision, as needed, according to interests, needs, maturity, given the number of children and the space and time involved.

Anthony Pelligrini (2011) wrote that, "Guided play is a synergistic learning process, in which learning continually oscillates between planned, teacher-enriched contexts and self-directed, emergent learning contexts over time. Guided play is a concept that deserves serious consideration by educators" (p. 3).

"WHY CAN'T WE PLAY?"

Despite data-driven evidence across disciplines that strongly supports the importance of play in early learning, socialization, and development, time for young children to play freely at home or school continues to diminish. In the current climate, play and learning are deemed antithetical. The whole-child approach has been replaced by a single-minded cognitive system. Dress up, kitchen settings, building blocks, and traditional free-play areas are being eliminated from early childhood classrooms and replaced by direct instruction and worksheets. Even recess and physical education classes in elementary schools are being reduced or cut from the children's school day because there is not enough time for lessons on reading and literacy, numeracy, and mathematics.[24]

Lack of opportunities to play extends beyond the classroom. When children get home from school, too many have no safe place to run, jump, swing, and play outside. Instead they remain locked indoors or they are transported for activities organized and directed by adults. The contributing factors to the demise of play are many; however, the fundamental shift away from playful learning systematically began with *A Nation at Risk* (1983). This federal report induced seismic pressure on school districts, administrators, and teachers to conform to a universal, standardized curriculum, high-stakes testing, and teacher accountability. The aftershocks of *A Nation at Risk*, No Child Left Behind, Race to the Top, and Common Core Standards continue unabated and remain destructive.

In the world of *Peanuts*, created by Charles Schultz, cartoonist and some say philosopher, Charlie Brown, his sister Sally, and Peppermint Patty struggle against the rigors of schooling. Not unlike real children today, Charlie Brown and his friends memorize facts, take tests, and lament their plight. Upon hearing that school is about to start up again, Sally says, "Not for me—I went last year." In a later episode, she wakes in a panic, "I can't go to school! I'm not ready! I don't where Italy is! I can't spell cavalry! Who was the father of Richard the Fiftieth?"

In *Reclaiming Childhood: Letting Children Be Children in Our Achievement-Oriented Society*, developmental psychologist William Crain analogizes the educational challenges of today's children with the fictional kids in *Peanuts*. His interpretation and analysis of Sally's persona is genuine. He writes:

> Sally Brown illustrates the conflict between the creative impulses of childhood and the demands of school. In this battle, Sally is holding her own. She keeps cracking jokes and coming up with new ideas. And this is what is so appealing about her. We don't appreciate Sally because of her success in school—because of any gold stars, good marks, or high achievement test scores. We appreciate her because she illustrates the unvanquished spirit of childhood struggling against an oppressive system. (p. 203)

Peppermint Patty excels at sports and games with enthusiasm and energy on the playground and at sports venues—outside the classroom. For Patty, the classroom is dull and difficult; her grades are a consistent D-minus. Her best qualities are undervalued in a restrictive academic environment; but Patty is a leader in the world of children. She's a kid's kid, one who loves to play and the first to get a game going. Her peers value her fairness, courage, and humor. To avoid answering questions for which she has no answer, Patty tries some of her best skills on her teacher. Of course, none of these attempts work to improve her academic performance. She gives up: "I'm getting dumber every day and it's all too embarrassing." Patty drops out of school, "I can't take it anymore."

Crain concludes, "There is no reason why a child must spend several hours a day struggling with tasks she finds overly difficult and meaningless and to come to feel inferior as a person because she performs poorly on them. Yet this is the situation countless children face" (p. 207).

If asked, Sally and Patty could tell you what's wrong with school. Saige Price, a seven-year-old in second grade at Briarwood Elementary School, Florham Park, New Jersey, did just that before the New Jersey State Board of Education. She began her presentation with why children need more time for free play, for exploring and playing with friends. "Instead," she said, "we spend most of our time just reading, doing math problems, taking math tests and reading tests."

Saige asked the policy makers a profound question and then answered it for them: "Is that all that matters to grown-ups? What about more lunch time, more time for violin, doing more creative stuff in art, dance, or musical theater, more gym time, or more time to learn what we want? What about creating our own problems?"

Her kindergarten year seems similar to Sally Brown's. Paige said:

> I remember when I was 5 years old, I told my mom that I did not want to take iReady. Whenever I got a low score I would have to go back to the computer lab until I got a higher score. I hated it. It should be against the law. I think kindergartners should not have to take any standardized test or practice standardized test like iReady. These tests are too hard for kindergartners.
>
> I remember being 5 and feeling mad and sad because the questions were always too hard for me. Every time I sat at the computer after I was done with the test, I would think to myself, "I stink! I am bad at this."

Paige appealed to the school board members for attention to children's basic needs:

> Have you ever been in a kids' lunch room at lunch time? If you go to many of these cafeterias, you will see there is hardly enough time to even eat. Many kids end up throwing their food away. Some of the teachers often ask us if we are sure we want to throw the food away

but many do anyway because we want to play for the few minutes we have. Out of all the hours we spend in school, we have the least amount of time being able to eat and play.[25]

Children know that they need to eat lunch, to play, make music and art, engage in dance, theater, and gym activities, and take part in their own learning. Saige Price knows that "If you want to fix schools you should ask kids, the teacher's helpers, and teachers."

NOTES

1. L. A. Custodero, C. Cali, A. Diaz-Donoso, "Tunes and Rhythms as Transitional Objects: Children's Spontaneous Musical Behaviors in the Subway." *Proceedings for the International Society for Music Education's Early Childhood Music Education Commission seminar*, Brasilia, Brazil, 2014.

2. University students enrolled in my music education courses for early childhood and elementary school majors.

3. Michael Polanyi, *Personal Knowledge: Towards a Post-Critical Philosophy*. Chicago: University of Chicago Press, 1958.

4. Notes from the website: "Professor Piaget wrote these comments after reading in manuscript Chapter 2 and excerpts from Chapter 6 of Vygotsky's *Thought and Language*. His comments were translated from the French by Anne Parsons; the translation was revised and edited by E. Hanfmann and G. Vakar.

5. Arrested for his outspoken views against the occupation of his country, Huizinga died in a Nazi prison.

6. Edward Holmes, *The Life of Mozart*. London: J. M. Dent, 1932. Holmes estimated 1789 as the date of this letter.

7. Water for infants (barley water) was a common feeding practice; sadly, few babies survived due to contaminated water.

8. Baptized Johannes Chrysostomus Wolfgangus Theophilus, January 28,1756.

9. Edward Holmes, *The Life of Mozart*. London: J. M. Dent, 1932.

10. It is likely, fond as he was in later years of comic, racy wordplay, and puns.

11. This exchange is sometimes called protocommunication or protoconversation. Colwyn Trevarthen, "Musicality and the Intrinsic Motive Pulse: Evidence from Psychobiology and Infant Communication." *Musicae Scientiae*, Special Issue, 1999/2000.

12. Laura Krauss Melmed, Ed Young, and Lee Lothrop, *The First Song Ever Sung*. New York: Lothrop, Lee & Shepard Books, 1993.

13. Donald Johanson and Maitland Edey, *Lucy: The Beginnings of Humankind*. New York: Simon & Schuster, 1981.

14. M. Papoušek, *Vom ersten Schrei zum ersten Wort* (1994); Translation quoted in *Dissanayake* (2000), "Antecedents of the Temporal Arts in Early Mother-Infant Interaction." In Nils L. Wallin, Bjorn Merker, and Steven Brow, eds., *The Origins of Music*. Cambridge: Massachusetts Institute of Technology, 2000.

15. Desmond Lewis, *The Human Zoo*. New York: McGraw-Hill, 2000. First published 1969.

16. Kenneth Page Oakley, *Man the Tool-Maker*. Chicago: University Press of Chicago, 1957.

17. Aleksei Stakhanova was a Russian coal miner recognized for overachieving hard work.

18. These findings are preliminary and have not been tested.

19. Teachers were present for safety supervision. Interestingly, the children did not seek their attention or assistance at any time during eight weeks (thirteen hours) of the study.

20. Use of the video camera was unobtrusive.

21. Each free-play session was scheduled and videotaped for thirty minutes.

22. This child was clever and effective, as when their hands are in the air they cannot play the instruments!

23. At Disney World's Animal Kingdom Park, there is a variety of drums set aside for anyone to play. Rarely have I seen adults play them, only children. What an interesting setting for studying children's drumming improvisations, interactions, and collaborations.

24. *New York Times*, February 19, 2013.

25. (www.washingtonpost.com/blogs/answer-sheet/wp/2015/01/17/test-weary-second-grader-schools-state-school-board-is-that-all-that-matters-to-grown-ups/).

Saige Price spent the winter break working on her presentation. Saige's mother helped organize her writing, but all the ideas were Saige's own.

THREE

Originality

The Voices of Children

*Every childhood has its talismans, the sacred objects that look innocuous
enough to the outside world, but that trigger an onslaught of vivid memories
when the grown child confronts them.*
—Steven Johnson

Known for the breadth of her intellect and interest in children's lives, Edith Cobb, in *The Ecology of Imagination in Childhood*, tells us that wonder is the genesis of knowledge and it originates in childhood. Researchers in psychology and child studies Dorothy Singer and Jerome Singer, in *The House of Make-Believe*, spoke about imagination in this way: "The concept of 'what might be'—being able to move in perception and thought away from the concrete given . . . and ultimately, to the purest realm of fantasy—is a touchstone of that miracle of human experience, the imagination" (p. 19).

In the following vignettes, two scientists, a musician, an entomologist, an anthropologist, and a mythologist describe the wonder of childhood and ways it influenced and sustained each one's identity and life's work. From his childhood's perspective, Sir Isaac Newton recalled his fascination with the natural world:

> I do not know what I may appear to the world; but to myself I seem to have been only like a boy playing on the seashore, and diverting myself in now and then finding a smoother pebble or a prettier shell than ordinary, while the great ocean of truth lay all undiscovered before me. (p. 88)

(Sir Isaac might have enjoyed American comedian, actor, and writer Steven Wright's amusing comment: "I have a large shell collection which I keep scattered on the beaches all over the world. Perhaps you've seen it.")

When children play, imagine, and create, they enter a private reality. In "a world apart" they find happy amusement, fanciful escapes, and passionate engagements that can shape a lifetime. In his biography, *My Young Years*, Arthur Rubinstein recalled his earliest memories of musical sound, singing, and playing the piano:

> My first musical impressions were formed by the lugubrious and plain-tive shrieks of factory sirens . . . and, the pleasant musical fare when gypsies would appear in our courtyard, singing and dancing. . . . There was also the singsong of Jewish old-clothes peddlers, of Russian ice-cream sellers, and Polish peasant women chanting the praises of their eggs, vegetables, and fruit. (p. 4)

As a toddler, Arthur was fascinated by sound and he amused his family with vocal imitations of factory ruckus and street cries. It was as though these random sounds were his means of communication. "I loved all these noises, and while nothing would induce me to utter a single word, I was always willing to sing—to imitate with my voice—any sound I heard, thus creating quite a sensation at home" (1973, p. 4). He explained that he continued being a human parrot for two years until his parents bought an upright piano for his two older sisters to take lessons. That's when he discovered the "divine instrument" (p. 4). In the same manner that Wolfgang listened to Nannerl's piano lessons, Arthur at about the same age or younger listened to his sisters' lessons. Arthur's talent and passion for playing soon gave him prominence at the keyboard. In *My Young Years*, Arthur wrote that when he was denied access to the piano, he resorted to yelling and crying as his only defenses, and that for him learning to master the keyboard was mere child's play. Pablo Picasso famously said, "All children are artists. The problem is how to remain an artist once he grows up." As a child, the evolutionary biologist E. O. Wilson was passionate about and loved the wonderful things he found in nature. He affirmed that play is one of the most important issues concerned with understanding human behavior. Cheekily, Wilson said, "Every kid has a bug period—I never grew out of mine."

Jane Goodall never forgot her "most cherished possession." In *Reason for Hope: A Spiritual Journey*, she recalls that her father gave her a large stuffed chimpanzee toy when she was little more than a year old. The toy was created to celebrate the birth of Jubilee, the first baby chimpanzee ever born at the London Zoo. Jane wrote that her so-named Jubilee "accompanied me on nearly all my childhood adventures. To this day old Jubilee is still with me, almost hairless from all the loving." From her childhood discoveries of insects and other living things to her scientific breakthroughs with the chimpanzees of Gombe, she exhibited the curiosity of a child, the spirituality of a seeker, the dedication of an environmentalist, and methodological reasoning of a scientist. When Goodall attracted attention and subsequently was trained by the eminent paleontologist Louis Leakey, her life's work was assured, and Jubilee remained her inspiration.

Be it known that a simple toy might for one child become a talisman and to another child only a material object. For Jane Goodall, the talisman was her Jubilee, and for Albert Einstein, it was a compass. "When I was a little boy my father showed me a small compass, and the enormous impression it made on me certainly played a role in my life." In an interview, October 26, 1929, he said, "Imagination is more important than knowledge. Knowledge is limited. Imagination encircles the world." Given this viewpoint, it is not surprising that when Albert was a young student, he rebelled against the rigidity of his schooling, especially rote learning and recitation. At age five, he threw a chair at a particularly surly teacher. Later, he commented that "[t]he spirit of learning and creative thought were lost in strict learning." There were erroneous reports that he was a poor academic student. It seems that one of his early teachers said, "Never will he get anywhere." Perhaps, it was the schooling that failed the endlessly curious Albert, not the other way around. Passion for science and music emerged in his early years and continued throughout his life. "We never cease to stand like curious children before the great Mystery into which we are born."[1]

Joseph Campbell was honored as a scholar and a beloved storyteller for bringing mythology into popular culture, especially through the PBS series *The Power of Myth with Bill Moyers*. Campbell recalled that at age seven, his father took him and his younger brother to Buffalo Bill's Wild West Show. Later he wrote that although the cowboys were the stars of the show, he "became fascinated, seized, and obsessed by the figure of a naked American Indian with his ear to the ground, a bow and arrow in his hand, and a look of special knowledge in his eyes." Arthur Schopenhauer, the philosopher, whose writings influenced Campbell, observed that:

> The experiences and illuminations of childhood and early youth become in later life the types, standards and patterns of all subsequent knowledge and experience, or as it were, the categories according to which all later things are classified—not always consciously, however. And so it is that in our childhood years the foundation is laid of our later view of the world, and there with as well of its superficiality or depth: it will be in later years unfolded and fulfilled, not essentially changed. (www.jcf.org)

Those quoted here were passionate about the piano, bugs, a stuffed toy chimp, a compass, and the image of a knowledgeable Native American tracker. For Eudora Welty, words were her passion. In *One Writer's Beginnings*, the author wrote about growing up with parents who owned many books and loved reading Mark Twain, Charles Dickens, Robert Lewis Stevenson, and other famous writers of the past and of their time. Eudora said this about her earliest recollection of the visual attraction of letters on the pages of her storybooks:

> My love of the alphabet, which endures, grew out of reciting it, but before that, out of seeing the letters on the page. In my own story books, before I could read them for myself, I fell in love with various winding, enchanted-looking initials drawn by Walter Crane at the heads of fairy tales. In "Once upon a time," an "O" had a rabbit running a treadmill, his feet upon flowers. When the day came, years later, for me to see the Book of Kells, all the wizardry of letters, initial, and word swept over me a thousand times over, and the illuminations, the gold, seemed a part of the word's beauty and holiness that had been there from the start. (p. 9)

In the next passage, she describes experiencing the word "moon":

> At around age six, perhaps, I was standing by myself in our front yard waiting for supper, just at that hour in a late summer day when the sun is already below the horizon and the risen full moon in the visible sky stops being chalky and begins to take on light. There comes the moment, and I saw it then when the moon goes from flat to round. For the first time it met my eyes as a globe. The word "moon" came into my mouth as though fed to me out of a silver spoon. Held in my mouth the moon became a word. It had the roundness of a Concord grape Grand Pa took off his vine and gave me to suck out of its skin and swallow whole, in Ohio.[2] (p. 10)

As a young child, Eudora's sensory and emotional experiences of letters and words were vivid and extraordinary. In a language of feeling, she described the enchantment of *seeing* letters on the page and the sensation of the word "moon" in her mouth. In the next passage, she refers to the lifelong experience of *hearing* the words as she writes and *listening* to them as she reads:

> Ever since I was first read to, then started reading to myself, there has never been a line read that I didn't hear. As my eyes followed the sentence, a voice was saying it silently to me. . . . It is to me the voice of the story or the poem itself. The cadence, whatever it is that asks you to believe, the feeling that resides in the printed word reaches me through the reader-voice. . . . My own words, when I am at work on a story, I hear too as they go, in the same voice that I hear when I read in books. When I write and the sound of it comes back to my ears, then I act to make changes. I have always trusted this voice. (pp. 11–12)
>
> . . . Learning stamps you with its moments. Childhood's learning is made up of moments. It isn't steady. It's a pulse. (p. 9)

Mary Chapin Carpenter, singer-songwriter, said after first reading *One Writer's Beginnings* that she "returned to the book countless times, for wisdom and inspiration, and for the rewards it offers to anyone who has ever felt the spark of creativity." Miss Welty told a story about the time she was "indeed carried to the window as an infant in arms and shown Halley's comet in my sleep." Moved by this tender story, Ms. Carpenter wrote a cradle-rocking song, a life-story song, a generational song, *When Halley Came to Jackson*.[3]

What might be discerned from the exceptional lives of Arthur Rubinstein, E. O. Wilson, Jane Goodall, Albert Einstein, Joseph Campbell, and Eudora Welty? There are no common elements or causality in the randomness of their genetics, happenstance of birthplace, chronological era, or cultural environment. However, the evolution of human biology suggests that as human infants we are more alike than different and what we as humans need to survive, thrive, and flourish is common across time, place, and culture. Why does this matter? Because what we *believe a child is like* guides how we interact with and think about children, how we prepare nurturing environments, and provide for their growth in every area of human potential. The manner in which we relate to children shapes the success of our teaching and, more importantly, their lives.

Anthropologist Ashley Montagu in the chapter "The Neotenous Traits of the Child," from his book *Growing Young* defines the basic behavioral needs of children. He writes, "Most of these needs are not even recognized in works on child growth and development." Among the neotenous traits he cites are: love and friendship; sensitivity; thinking soundly, knowing, learning, and working; curiosity, wonder, playfulness, imagination, and creativity; open-mindedness, flexibility, experimentation, and resilience; enthusiasm, joy, compassion, honesty, and trust, and the need for song and dance.

The theory of neoteny in human development concerns the retention of childlike traits into adulthood, not only of artists and geniuses, but also the rest of us. Conceptually, the idea of neoteny emerged in the nineteenth century and was studied by scientists in zoology, embryology, biology, paleontology, anatomy, anthropology, social psychology, and psychiatry. In *Growing Young*, Montagu explains that neoteny in human biological evolution and human behavior accounts for evolutionary advantages that need not disappear as we grow older. He said that growing *young*, rather than growing *old*, is the natural order of humankind, "The idea is to die young as late as possible." When asked, "What, precisely, are those traits of childhood behavior that are so valuable and that tend to disappear gradually as human beings grow older?" Montagu replied, "We only have to watch children to see them clearly displayed."

By way of example, consider the puckish playfulness of young Peter Ustinov, from his autobiography, *Dear Me*: "I was a motorcar to the dismay of my parents. . . . I switched on in the morning, and only stopped being a car at night when I reversed into bed and cut off the ignition" (p. 68).[4] Evidenced by *Dear Me* (1977) and *Quotable Ustinov* (1995), this witty author scintillates and entertains as an actor, director, playwright, novelist, opera director, and mimic. He recalls himself "as the one-child cabaret of vocal mimicry, scattering pedestrians with his sudden, blaring 'horns and brakes.'" In later years, he recorded a cacophony of sounds on *Voices and Noises of Peter Ustinov* and *The Grand Prix of Gibraltar*. Sir Peter delighted children and un-grown-up adults with recordings of imaginative narration and storytelling: *Peter Ustinov Reads the Orchestra, Peter and the Wolf, Carnival of the Animals,* and *Peter Ustinov Tells the Tales of Barbar the Elephant, The Little Tailor,* and *The Story of Blackbeard's Ghost.*

BEING *WITH* CHILDREN: CHILD WATCHING

A teacher is a professional observer of children—a child watcher. It is our responsibility to pay special attention to children's growth, development, and learning; and to see each child as that child needs to be seen— through the lens of compassion and respect. Children with hurt feelings want comfort and compassion. Children who come to school from chaos at home hope for understanding and patience. Sadly, for some children their emotional life goes unnoticed. Have you ever heard anyone say, "I can tell you about a school from the moment I go inside"? The sights, sounds, and, yes, smells give you a feeling about what it's like to be a child or teacher there. Even in schools that are less than welcoming, there are individual classrooms where every child is wanted, honored, and cared for. Those teachers are remembered and called by name even after many years have passed. Here are some thoughts from theologian Henri J. M. Nouwen about being with children:

> Our children are our most important guests, who enter into our home, ask for careful attention, stay for a while and then leave to follow their own way. Children are strangers whom we have to get to know. They have their own style, their own rhythm, and their own capacity for good and evil. What parents [and I believe teachers] can offer is a home, a place that is receptive but also has the safe boundaries within which their children can develop and discover what is helpful and what is harmful. There, children can ask questions without fear and can experiment with life without taking the risk of rejection. There they can be encouraged to listen to their own inner selves and to develop the freedom that gives them the courage to leave home and travel on. The hospitable home indeed is the place where father, mother, and children can reveal their talents to each other, become present to each other as members of the same human family and support each other in their common struggles to live and make a life.[5]

GOODNESS OF CHILDREN

Children are forgiving. In more than one instance, I found that I had admonished the wrong child or chastised another unfairly. [*Note to self: Take time to get it right. Don't ignore your mistake and just move on.*] When I failed them, I said, "I'm sorry," or "I misspoke," or "Pardon me, I thought you were the one misbehaving." When I was wrong, they forgave me. Children are honest and they expect fairness from each other—and their teachers. Because they are sensitive to our every move and emotion, children help us learn how to be with and teach them by how they see *us*. That means if we are self-aware, we may discover that it is *we* who contribute to children's unrest and unruliness.

Checklist: What was I saying that they didn't understand? What was the emotional tone of my voice? Did I seem pleasant or irritable? Did my eye contact or lack of it and my close or distant proximity to the students influence their behavior? Did my gestures and body language convey openness or stiffness? Did I appear comfortably relaxed or tense? Do the children know and feel that I am caring and interested in them? Do I recognize and delight in children's humor? Never have I felt more capable than when I've righted a wrong with a classroom full of children watching me apologize.

Do you know a child like Milo? He was a new kindergarten student and one of many in his class who had difficulty settling in. When invited to play drums, he blossomed with dedication and new sense of purpose. Whenever he saw me outside the music room, he asked, "Do you remember me? I played the drums really good!" "Of course, I do. Yes, you did!" Milo's contributions to his music classes were exemplary and exceptional for a five-year-old. He remembered practically every word I spoke in class about the music we played and the different ways to play a variety of instruments. Often Milo offered suggestions, and a few times, he shushed a noisy classmate with, "I am trying to listen here."

One day he was "in trouble" with the after-care staff. On the way to my music room, I noticed Milo sitting in a corner of the huge noisy cafeteria—alone. "What's wrong?" I asked. He said, holding back tears, "It's not fair . . . he hit *me*, see? I'm trying to control my anger." We sat on the floor and talked. Milo saw a tiny baby lizard and touched it gently. "I think he wants his mother and father" [and Milo as well]. "I think you're right. You're a good guy, Milo." This child struggles for self-control with superhero strength despite unfairness. He's aware when he's getting angry and works very hard to contain it. Milo exerts more effort and discipline than most adults in need of understanding. Children need empathy.

I met Artie in my second year of teaching music in a remote, poverty-stricken area of southern Ohio, white Appalachia. He came to school often without shoes and in clothes he'd worn for days. Artie was repeating the first grade. But there was a light in his young, bright eyes. He seemed hopeful. One day I asked his class if they knew a song they'd like to sing before the end of our music lesson. Except for Artie, all the other first-grade children remained shyly quiet. Artie volunteered to sing his song; he began freely improvising a song about riding with his brother on his motorcycle. Artie sang and sang enthusiastically about this adventure; his was a rambling, melismatic, passionate song.

His classmates did not know what to make of him, especially since they heard his teachers label him a failure "just like his brothers." All the children joined me in applauding and complimenting Artie. In those days, music teachers produced Christmas programs in public schools. When his first-grade teacher heard I asked Artie to sing the angel solo, she took me aside and insisted I remove him from the play. I was young. I said no. All went well. The children and I were proud of their performances. In the spring that year, I gave Artie an important role in our musical performance of *The Rabbit Who Wanted Red Wings*. Many years later, I remember Artie and the lessons I learned from him—trust, resilience, honesty, enthusiasm, creativity, hope, and the goodness of children.

Children are sincere and their emotions are pure. If we let them, they will show us the advantages of innocence. A tender seven-year-old child told me about her new friend. "We are just alike. She's very sensitive and cries easily, like me. Actually, she's my style. She's my flavor. She is adopted, but she looks like her mother. Her parents are divorced. Her sister and brother got divorced too." (This was the child's way of saying that the children were separated from the family they knew.)

Children are hopeful and courageous. Yolanda at age eleven had a wonderful voice and a desperate desire to sing. Not a popular girl, angry and poor in demeanor and attitude, she was a difficult child in and out of my music room. One day after class, I asked her:

> *What music do you like?*
> "Mariah Carey."
> *Is there a particular song?*
> "Hero."
> *Would you sing it for me?*

What followed was transformational for Yolanda and for me. That day we met in the music room after school. With her permission, we made a videotape of her singing so she could see and hear herself. She was harsh with self-criticism and defeat, but as she accepted my encouragement and suggestions, her confidence swelled. She asked if we could keep having lessons. When she gained enough courage, she sang for her uncharitable classmates. They cheered! Yolanda had found her voice and a *hero* of her own.[6]

INFLUENCES OF GREAT EDUCATORS

The great educators of the past believed in the goodness of children. They asserted that teachers were responsible for creating the environments to nurture children's goodness. Just like those teachers, *we* are called to truly care about the children we serve. Educators credited with establishing the foundations of modern educational thought and practices were well educated in philosophy, science, and medicine. They were dedicated to social change for the good of all, and remarkably most of them were devoutly religious: John Amos Comenius (b. 1592), Jean-Jacque Rousseau (b. 1712), Johann Heinrich Pestalozzi (b. 1746), Friedrich Wilhelm Fröebel (b. 1782), John Dewey (b. 1859), and Maria Montessori (b. 1870).

A thread of learning connects all who study the acknowledged work of others, scholar to scholar, and teacher to student. Isaac Newton said, "If I have seen further than others, it is by standing *upon the shoulders of giants.*" Alfred North Whitehead, mathematician and philosopher was an intellectual giant of the early twentieth century. Whitehead was born in Ramsgate, Kent, England, in 1861. He entered Trinity College, Cambridge, in 1880 with a scholarship in mathematics; only four years later he was elected a fellow in mathematics. He acquired distinguished awards and recognition for his seminal works in mathematics, logic, science, metaphysics, theology, and education. In 1924 Whitehead was appointed professor of philosophy at Harvard University and he remained in that position until retirement in 1937.

Shortly after Whitehead's death in 1947, Justice Felix Frankfurter wrote a letter to the *New York Times* in honor of his friend. Excerpted comments illumine the spirit and character of this great scholar:

> From the time he came to Harvard in 1924, he infused an understanding of interdependence among the various disciplines, to use the common jargon. For all who came within the range of his infectious personality, arid professionalism was quickened into exhilarating meaning and the universe expanded. Such was the quiet, almost shy magic of his qualities that his influence imperceptibly but quickly permeated the whole university.
>
> . . . Professor Whitehead had a benign and beautiful presence, a voice and diction that made music of English speech, humor that lighted dark places, humility that made the foolish wiser and evoked the wisdom of the taciturn.[7]

Some teachers may never know the reach of their influence. A music history professor in my sophomore year assigned *The Aims of Education and Other Essays* by Alfred North Whitehead (1929–1963). He told us Whitehead was one of the great thinkers of the twentieth century and we would do well to learn how to write from his example—ideas expressed with clarity and brevity. Whitehead's book was required reading; otherwise, I might not have discovered it.

Reading Whitehead gave me an informed and passionate foundation for my active life of learning and teaching. The works of his brilliant student Susanne Langer, *Philosophy in a New Key* (1942) and *Feeling and Form* (1953), introduced and stimulated my interest in nondiscursive forms of meaning and insight into the "significance of music."

In the first sentence of the first essay in *The Aims of Education and Other Essays*, "The Aims of Education," Whitehead presented his overarching thesis: "Culture is activity of thought and receptiveness to beauty and humane feeling. Scraps of information have nothing to do with it." Later in this essay, he defined education succinctly, gracefully, and with an unforgettable metaphor, *You may not divide the seamless coat of learning*:

> What education has to impart is an intimate sense for the power of ideas, for the beauty of ideas, and for the structure of ideas, together with a particular body of knowledge which has peculiar reference to the life of the being possessing it. (p. 23)

"In training a child to activity of thought," Whitehead warned that teachers must beware of "inert ideas," meaning ideas that are not being "utilized, tested, or thrown into fresh combinations." Tested? Whitehead refers to testing *ideas*, generative ideas, those worthy of examination that lead to: (a) knowledge by thinking, explaining, organizing, analyzing, and problem solving; and (b) proficiency when students master skills and apply them to discover that which they really want to know.

Whitehead did not approve of external testing; that is, tests created by anyone other than the student's own teacher or lessons designed by anyone other than the student's teacher. He would certainly decry high-stakes, standardized testing. Instead of immersion in rich, interesting, and meaningful learning experiences, today's students, trapped inside a virtual classroom "test tube," encounter dead-end ideas and endure mind-numbing practice sessions. Active thought cannot survive in an arid and barren learning environment—neither can animate learners.

Whitehead reasoned that lack of attention to student's intellectual growth is a main source of the "wooden futility in education." He posited three stages of learning—romance, precision, and generalization:

> The stage of romance is the stage of first apprehension. The subject matter has the vividness of novelty; it holds within itself unexplained connexions with possibilities half-disclosed by glimpses and half-concealed by the wealth of material. In this stage, knowledge is not dominated by systematic procedure. . . . Romantic emotion is essentially the excitement consequent on the transition from the bare facts to the first realisations of the import of their unexplained relationships. (pp. 28–29)

Romance is a marvelous similitude applied to a young child's "falling in love" with learning. Children are seekers of novelty, delight, and joy, and they are full of curiosity, indicating that their pursuits are truly born of fascination and *romance*. For Arthur Rubinstein, his love was the piano and music. Edward Osborne (E. O.) delighted in bugs, and Jane hugged the toy chimp Jubilee all her life. A small compass charmed Albert Einstein. Joseph Campbell had a passion for storytelling, and Eudora Welty was wooed by words.

According to Whitehead's hypothesis, the stage of romance is subsumed by precision, the "stage of grammar, the grammar of language, the grammar of science." Furthermore, he explains the unalterable connection between the passages of learning, of romance and precision:

> It is evident that a stage of precision is barren without a previous stage of romance; unless there are facts, which have already been vaguely apprehended in their broad generality, the previous analysis is an analysis of nothing. It is simply a series of meaningless statements about bare facts, produced artificially and without any further relevance. I repeat that in this stage we do not merely remain within the circle of the facts elicited in the romantic epoch. The facts of romance have disclosed ideas with possibilities of wide significance, and in this stage of precise progress we acquire other facts in a systematic order, which thereby form both a disclosure and an analysis of the general subject-matter of the romance. (pp. 29–30)

There is a rhythmic, yet nonlinear, confluence of learning throughout Whitehead's stages of romance, precision, and generalization. Whitehead identifies the third stage of intellectual growth as the stage of generalization. This brings his theory of learning full circle. "It is a return to romanticism with added advantage of classified ideas and relevant technique. It is the fruition, which has been the goal of precise training. It is the final success" (p. 30).

Considering the current era of standardization, I argue that the *romance* of learning has in all ways been replaced by the relentless drive for *precision*. What does this mean in the education, specifically music education, of children and their teachers? It means returning *romance* to preschool, kindergarten, and first grade where children's play replaces worksheets, and music, dance, drama, storytelling, and art become the new academics for the young.

In the romance of learning, children explore found or teacher-prepared materials for constructing playscapes and soundscapes. Musical drawings, manipulatives, props, and costumes contribute to children's discoveries, stimulate story making, and advance their literacy skills. Schedules suited to young children's natural rhythm would replace rigid, compartmentalized routines to allow for long periods of uninterrupted learning and engagement. Implementation of music-across-the-curriculum strategies would extend children opportunities for sustained interest and provide their teachers a distinctive means of organizing instruction.

ECOLOGY OF LEARNING

From an ecological psychologist's perspective, children and their environments are mutually adaptive systems that may enhance or limit the child's emotional growth, cognitive development, and learning. Everything and everyone in the child's environment influence the child's behavior: adults and peers; events and objects; and the structure and ambience of the setting. Kurt Lewin (1933) theorized that behavior is a function of the state of the person and of the psychological environment (B=f (PE). Roger Barker (1968) asserted that he and his research associates could predict some aspects of children's behavior more adequately from knowledge of the behavior characteristics of environments than from behavior tendencies of particular children.

American developmental psychologist Urie Bronfenbrenner (1979) used the metaphor of nested Russian dolls to conceptualize the ecology of human development. He identified the innermost level as the child's home environment, next the classroom, then the outer setting, the society at large. Ecological psychologist James Garbarino (1989), following Bronfenbrenner, explained development in context in his own words:

> Thus development is the drawing of a social map, a map brought to life in behavior as it arises and is understood by the individual. The individual proceeds with the drawing of this map in counterpoint to social experience that arises from the nested social systems of family, school, neighborhood, church, society and culture.[8] (p. 19)

In other words, *it takes a whole village to raise a child.*[9] For too many children who attend run-down schools, live in abandoned neighborhoods, suffer poverty and broken families, and succumb to a culture of violence, their village is dysfunctional and injurious. Can a dying village be saved? I know one . . .

After the neighborhood school closed, the village deteriorated—until *a hero came along.* When he grew up there, kids walked to school, parents had pride in students' excellence in sports and music, and everyone celebrated high school graduations. He never left the neighborhood where generations of families worked the same sugarcane fields and took care of each other's children.

After the school closed in compliance with the desegregation policies of the 1970s, students were bussed to seventeen different schools across town. By the end of the next decade, drugs and crime had gained control of this and many other neighborhoods in cities small and big. Our hero started a movement that ultimately saved the village. He organized a local chapter of a national organization, MAD DADS (Men Against Drugs Defending Against Destruction And Social Disorder). Determined and respected, the men walked the tough streets until others joined to help. Partnerships were created with city government, children's organizations, and youth-development programs.

More than one dream came true when a local philanthropist made a sizeable financial commitment to build a new school. Three years after it opened, supported in part by the Art and Sara Jo Kobacker Foundation, I became the first full-time music teacher for kindergarten through grade four. This is the story of my time there; it is one of heartbreaking challenges and life-affirming rewards.

PEDAGOGY OF CULTURE

It seems to me that culture is more important than race when a white teacher teaches black children. With compassioned enlightenment, Vivian Paley described how she discovered her own insecurities in understanding the black children in her kindergarten. In *White Teacher*, Paley brings the reader into her classroom as she tells of struggles with children's and her own issues about race, color, culture, and ethnicity. From the beginning, Paley kept a journal in the form of scripts detailing each day's conflicts, failures, and successes. Her reflections, knowledge, and insights are recorded in her many books, which have inspired and guided my work, especially *You Can't Say You Can't Play, Bad Guys Don't Have Birthdays, The Kindness of Children*, and *A Child's Work: The Importance of Fantasy Play*. Paley was awarded a MacArthur Fellowship, a so-called "Genius Grant," in 1989.

Scholar, author, and authority on urban education, Lisa Delpit accepted a MacArthur Fellowship in 1990 and received national acclaim for her work. In *Other People's Children: Cultural Conflict in the Classroom* (1995), she wrote:

> If we are to successfully educate all of our children, we must work to remove the blinders of stereotypes, monocultural instructional methodologies, ignorance, social distance, biased research, and racism. Yes, if we are to be successful at educating diverse children, we must accomplish the Herculean feat of developing this clear-sightedness, for in the words of a wonderful Native Alaskan educator: "In order to teach you, I must know you." (pp. 182–83)

The corollary to knowing others is knowledge of oneself.[10] The following personal narratives provide the backdrop for my evolving awareness of self-to-other-to-self. It takes courage to be a teacher, especially in times of social change. Schools mirror society like a canary in the coalmine.

A Point in Time: John F. Kennedy

The media reported the events surrounding the president's assassina-
tion without hype or hysteria. The live television broadcasts showed the
tragedy to every American viewer. On that day, I was a student teacher
conducting eighty-six students in a middle school chorus. When the news
came over the school intercom that the president had been assassinated,
loud cheers reverberated throughout the school. Horrified, I walked out
of the classroom, out of the school, and out of town. For the next few days
I watched the tragedies and funeral live on television. After a while, I
went to the ocean for solitude.

A Point in Time: Martin Luther King Jr.

During the civil rights movement, I taught music in an elementary
school in suburban Atlanta. When Martin Luther King Jr. was assassinated, a shocked nation grieved. On the day of his funeral in Atlanta, city
schools in that city were dismissed, but the schools in my district, DeKalb
County, remained open. The principal and my fellow teachers were
shocked and saddened by King's tragic death—except for one. He was
angry and bragged about how he and his friends went to Birmingham,
Alabama, where King was incarcerated. They poured slop and other dis-
tasteful matter into his cell. That day the principal came to my classroom
and told me to leave for the rest of the day. He worried that tension was
high, and my colleague had focused his anger at me. "I don't think you
are safe. Please go home now." I picked up my daughter from day care,
went home, and watched the nonviolent marches down Peachtree Street
on television. Later that same school year, Robert F. Kennedy was assassinated in Los Angeles.

A Point in Time: Kent State University

My next elementary music position was in southern Ohio near Cincin-
nati during the student protests against the Vietnam War. At the teachers' lunch table on May 4, 1970, news came that the Ohio National Guard
was deployed to Kent State University. The conversation among the
teachers and principal was chilling. Except for me, all were unanimous in
support of the military action against the student protestors. In those
days, teachers had lunch in the cafeteria with the students. Did the children nearby hear the teacher-talk that day? Perhaps they did not hear or
understand that only 244 miles away there were four dead and nine
wounded Kent State students who, according to their teachers, "got what
they deserved."

I did not return the following year, instead I applied for and was
offered several university positions in the United States, but when an

offer came from Canada, I accepted. It seemed to me that three times I had been out of place, in the wrong place at the wrong time. Like a pseudo Forrest Gump, I had been a witness to historic events and people that had changed my life and my country.

WHEN CHILDREN HURT

Conflicts in classrooms are unlimited and unalike; so too are the tools to solve them. Confounding our best efforts and expectations, a crisis erupts, or students have meltdowns. In the heat of the moment with no time to think, we act instinctively. Let me give you an example that happened in my kindergarten music class.

Upon entering the classroom, a little girl was provoked by another student. She flew into a rage and began hitting him. Quickly, and without a word of warning, the rest of the class jumped in, surrounded them, and started yelling, "FIGHT! FIGHT!" Fearing the children's safety, I broke through the group and pulled the little girl away. Blinded by rage, she began kicking and hitting me. When she slowed down from exhaustion, I asked her to please sit down. The rest of the children calmed down until their not-so-musical class ended and their classroom teacher came for them.

Having sustained multiple bruises and abrasions, I went to the school nurse's office for some ice—and there was my sad little friend. I asked, "Are you okay?" She nodded. It seemed all right to try to reach and comfort her, so I asked if she liked dolls . . . and music, just yes and no questions. She began to cry, and so did I. She wanted to see my arms and legs. I said, "I'm okay, too." After the little girl left to go home, the nurse told me, "That was the most beautiful thing I've ever witnessed." The principal said, "Well, that's the end of our music teacher." But I stayed; there were more lessons waiting for me. Lessons that would test my teaching skills and yet confirm my personal belief that acceptance and compassion are crucial to the quality of all our lives, children and adults, at school, at home, in our neighborhood and our village.

There were many hurt children in my school who acted out with angry disrespect and defiance toward their peers and teachers, including me. They engaged in taunting, name-calling, and hostile behavior that disrupted and often destroyed the learning environment. Abusive language by children cannot be tolerated any more than physical abuse. For the sake of the children's emotional, social, and moral development, teachers must not allow, ignore, or give in to verbal abuse. When a student called me "white cracker," it didn't harm me, but it would harm the angry child who said it and the others who heard it if I did not acknowledge the insult. This is how it happened:

The fourth-grade class that entered the music room appeared much more mature than their years. They were aggressive, noisy, and scuffed their shoes, making marks on the newly polished floor. As she came in, she looked at me and said, "Don't look at me, you white cracker!" The others laughed and booed her—and me. Once all were seated and calmed down, I said, "Before we have music today, I've got something to say. It is not okay to call me names—or anybody else." As I walked through the rows of students, I said, "I know I'm white. Just look . . . at my face, my hands and arms. Do you understand I didn't choose my color? I was born this way. Just as you are like you are." Amazingly, the students sat quietly, listened to every word, and watched my every move. I continued:

Let me tell you a story. When I was a college student flying home for Christmas, a big winter storm hit the Deep South; it was colder in Alabama than Alaska and the snow was deeper. My plane was forced down in Muscle Shoals, Alabama, far from my destination. The passengers on board were white businessmen in dark suits, a young black girl, and me. The landing was very scary, the plane shook in the high winds and the wings began icing up. The pilot announced that we would be transported to a local hotel and that there would be no flights until the next day.

At the hotel, we stood in line as the hotel clerk checked us into our rooms. Just ahead of me was the young black girl. The hotel clerk said, "You can't stay here." I pushed in and asked, "Why not?" He repeated, "She can't stay here. It's our policy." I argued back. The other passengers heard me, but no one spoke up. Then, an elderly black man who worked at the hotel as a porter (his job was to carry people's luggage to their rooms) spoke to me and said, "Miss, I have a family for this young girl to stay with." It seemed to me she'd be more comfortable in a private home than in this hotel. I went on to my room and later came down to the dining room for supper.

There were a lot of stares and whispers from the white hotel staff while I ate. The black kitchen staff peeked at me through the kitchen-door window. I suppose they too had heard that I caused a big fuss. The next morning, I phoned my parents to tell them that I'd get whatever transportation I could to get home. So, I packed up, checked out, and went down to the hotel lobby for news of transportation—whether any cars, trains, or airplanes were moving. Unfortunately, the airport was still closed and cars were stranded, blocking highways for miles.

Remember the porter who took care of the young black girl? Well, he came to me, ever so quietly, and said, "Miss, I have a taxi for you to get to the train station, and you can get connections to get home." The only cars moving that morning were taxis. This kind gentleman carried my luggage and led me to a private taxi operated by black folk for black folk, and the driver took me to the train station. As I left the hotel, I noticed that the businessmen were waiting for transportation.

Why do you think a black man helped a white girl get home? Why do you think a white girl would care about a black girl's safety and respectful treatment? It was the right thing to do. You can do the right thing too. Will you do the right thing when you see injustice if it's aimed at you or others—whether they look like you or not?

Later that day after school, the girl came back to see me. I invited her to come into my small office for privacy; she sat down in a chair facing me. She didn't say a word, but began to cry. I cried too. I held her hands and we sat together with tears running down our faces for quite a long time. Without a word, she looked at me . . . and left. After that day we had a silent understanding of mutual respect—*though not a word was spoken.*[11]

PEDAGOGY OF POSSIBILITY: SETTING THE ENVIRONMENT

Many music teachers face overwhelming challenges such as those described here. Working through difficulties requires more than rules. Setting the environment and attending to the ambience of the classroom effectively influences behavior from the time students arrive at the classroom door, how they are greeted and seated, and the placement of musical equipment and instruments. The following account describes solutions specific to my music room. You may not have a similar classroom setting, but you can apply the principles of organization for optimum learning and teaching.

The music room was huge and equipped with a full Yamaha Piano Lab, an acoustic piano, and individual student chairs. In addition to my collection of drums and small percussion instruments, the Community Foundation purchased additional instruments and teaching materials. The daily schedule included six classes and a planning period. Given the school's small enrollment, all students received music, art, and physical education once a week. Before students arrived, the cluttered and abandoned music room needed rearranging. The Yamaha keyboards, tables, and electronic hookups were moved from the middle of the room to the perimeter in a U-shape in order to open an area to situate a CD player, musical instruments, and teaching materials. Chairs were placed in one half of the room in theater-style rows, spaced far apart side to side and front to back, five rows with five seats in each row. This arrangement gave students more personal space and ensured eye contact with each one. Large, colorful instructional music posters were displayed around the classroom and a whiteboard was placed at the entrance announcing topics for "Music Today." The hallway leading into the classroom allowed the students to come inside and remain in line as each one was greeted and seated one at a time. Thoughtful preparation of the environment facilitated learning, organization, order, positive student behavior, and consistent procedures.

PEDAGOGY OF POSSIBILITY: CUSTOMIZING THE CURRICULUM[12]

Maintaining the learning environment depends on meaningful music content, engaging activities, and lessons designed for the particular student population we teach. All students in my school were of African descent; they lived in the same neighborhood, close to school, and nearly all were African-American children. A small number of Haitian-American children regularly arrived at our school, and in the ensuing years, a few Hispanic children were enrolled. The African-American students were energetic bordering on hyperactive and their response to music was immediate and visceral. Given the new language and cultural differences, the Creole-speaking children were shy and quiet and were frequently singled out as objects of ridicule. It was a challenge to create music-learning experiences that captured all students' attention, encouraged good behavior, and sustained participation.

All students loved to play instruments. For that reason, they were encouraged to *act as if* they wanted to play: "If you obey the music rules, you get to play the instruments. If you do not obey, you do not get to play." Once they were convinced this rule was nonnegotiable, "Obey, you play" was all that was needed. It became a mantra for their cooperation. As children entered the music room, each child was asked, "Do you want to play today?" "Yes." "What do you have to do first?" "Obey." Soon after they were seated, one or two students were invited to go to one of the electronic keyboards. "You can put on your headphones, turn on the keyboard, and practice," which the students interpreted as "mess around."

As they learned more about playing, they came to understand "practice," "improvise," and "compose." In each lesson, "ready" children were first to the keyboards until all had an instrument to play and listened to a brief demonstration of the keyboard functions, voice, style, and percussion. [*Note to self: Don't talk too much.*] In later lessons, students learned how to use the percussion setting and improvise rhythmic "conversations" with a keyboard partner. Each time students grew restless and off-task, a new and more challenging idea was introduced. With a minimum of talk, individuals were called on to "show your work to all of us." Some did not progress beyond messing around, but most liked to perform musical Question and Answer with their keyboard partners. As students improved, they learned how to produce a short rhythm pattern and use it to accompany their own rap. If they couldn't or wouldn't try to rap freestyle, they used short rhymes or verses they knew. One example was a rap-song by LL Cool J and En Vogue, "Who's Afraid of the Big Bad Wolf?" The rhythms and rhymes were easy to imitate and lots of fun. Students learned the refrain by chanting and clapping rhythms before trying it out on keyboards:

Who's afraid of the big bad wolf?
The big bad wolf, the big bad wolf?
Who's afraid of the big bad wolf?
Three little piggy-wigs!
(Some children added) *Not ME!*

The following four examples are by second and third graders who improvised their own raps and reluctantly wrote them down (they said they'd rather just play). Here is the first example:

I am rappin on the mike
That girl tite
My dog name is Spike
I said
You want to ride my bike

Second:

When I was in Kingrator
My friends say is cool to learn
how to read write and tie on shoes
The first grade was harder with
all that homework to do
The 3 grade is way harder

Third:

To the dumpster to house
I called the rat and the mouse
And throw them out my house.
Sitting on 23's counting my cheese.
That girl so fin she blow my mine
All I had in my pock[et] was a 1.99.
Sitting on 23's counting my cheese
They said what I had in my head was pease.

Fourth:

Once I was afrade I was testafied
And think how I would live without you by my side
And then I spend so many night
And think how can you do me wrong
But I was strong
And I learned how to get along

DRUM TALK, NOT PEOPLE TALK

Because students really wanted to play, they accepted the idea that talking destroys drumming. As with all music-teaching strategies, success depends on preparation and presentation for the students you teach. You may wish to seek differing materials and workshops for strategies and approaches to drumming and/or develop your own teaching techniques and procedures for drum groups. In my classroom, students were taught to follow a practice routine of clapping rhythm patterns: short, simple patterns for students to "copy me, like this, my turn, your turn." Once they caught on, they liked the difficulty of playing longer phrases with combinations of dynamic and tempo variations. Each student's abilities to maintain attention and accuracy received praise and encouragement. When a student was selected to be the leader, everyone else paid attention and wanted a turn. The next instructional step involved transferring these systematic rhythmic procedures to the drum circle. There was no need for people talk—including mine.

Drum Talk evolved as the students' best-liked music activity. As their listening and playing skills improved, they were offered more freedom and greater challenges in exploring, improvising, and performing with conga, tubano, djembe, and bongo drums. They were surprised to learn that African drums could really talk. "Do you know that many African languages such as Yoruba, Ashanti, and Igbo are tonal languages?"

I continued: "This means the sounds of their spoken words had a kind of singing quality. Somewhere back in time, some very imaginative person or persons invented a drum capable of copying the way they spoke, making it possible to send and receive messages across long distances. Here's how: They selected a tree log of the right size, cut it in half, hollowed out the inside, then carved slits of different lengths on the top, similar to bars on a xylophone. The "bars" played with stick-mallets produced the tones needed to communicate messages. Clever, don't you think?"

With replicas of two slit-log drums, we explored "talking" and began sending "messages" to one another. Students were captivated by the novelty of their drumming experiences and wanted to keep on playing. Encouraged by their interest in authentic drumming traditions, they were eager to listen to the album *Circle of Drums* by the brilliant African drum master Babatunde Olatunji. Students were fascinated and inspired by his technical virtuosity and ingenious musical ideas, asking "How'd he do that?" Just the question a teacher wants to hear. *They want to know—they really want to know!*

MUSIC OF MOTHER AFRICA

Students were interested to learn that during the time of slavery, drumming was forbidden throughout the slave states except in and around the city of New Orleans. I asked:

Why do you think slaves were forbidden to own or play drums?
"The slaves could send messages that nobody understood but them."
Exactly. Without their drums, they made rhythms with their hands and feet, but those sounds couldn't go as far as drum sounds.

Children in my school knew very little about their African heritage or how their ancestors' music, stories, dance, and songs built a cultural bridge over time and across oceans; or that their people survived slavery, and a century later led a political movement that changed unjust laws and moved the United States to greater equality. I taught children field songs and sacred songs that expressed the pain and sorrow of slavery and the hope of escape and freedom:

> *Take this hammer and carry it to the Captain,*
> *Take this hammer and carry it to the Captain,*
> *Take this hammer and carry it to the Captain,*
> *Tell him I'm gone. Tell him I'm gone.*

> *Sometimes I feel like a motherless child,*
> *Sometimes I feel like a motherless child,*
> *Sometimes I feel like a motherless child,*
> *A long way from home, a long way from my home.*

The younger students liked songs about trains, songs that were easy to learn and invited rhythmic movement, rhythmic accompaniment with instruments, and vocal train sounds:

> (Refrain)
> *Get on board, little children,*
> *Get on board, little children,*
> *Get on board, little children,*
> *There's room for many a-more.*

> *The gospel train's a-coming —*
> *I see it close at hand.*
> *I hear the car wheels rumbling*
> *And rolling through the land.*
> (Refrain)
> *I hear the train a-coming —*
> *She's coming round the curve.*
> *She's loosen'd all her steam and brakes*
> *And straining every nerve.*
> (Refrain)
> *The fare is cheap and all can ride —*
> *The rich and poor are there.*

No second class aboard this train
No difference in the fare.

Get on board little children,
Get on board little children,
Get on board little children,
There's room for many a-more.

Singing and dramatizing "Follow the Drinking Gourd" taught students the significance of the North Star and the Big Dipper constellation and how it guided slaves to make their way northward. We learned that they waded through rivers and streams, slept in the daytime, moved forward at night, and depended on white people and free black people to feed and hide them until they reached freedom. We learned about Harriet Tubman and Sojourner Truth and how they made countless dangerous journeys to lead their people out of slavery. In addition to "The Gospel Train," we sang "Swing Low, Sweet Chariot" and Little Red Caboose" and found hidden meanings in the lyrics. For example, "home" meant destination of a safe haven; "train" and "chariot" symbolized the Underground Railroad, and "over Jordan" often referred to the Ohio River, north of which was free territory. We read *Sweet Clara and the Freedom Quilt* (1993) and learned how women and girls sewed messages into patchwork quilts and hung them outside to warn about trouble, to tell of plans for escapes, and to show maps to guide their friends and neighbors northward. *Unspoken: A Story from the Underground Railroad* (2012) is a beautiful children's book that tells a story about a little slave girl and the friend who saved her. This powerful story, illustrated with images in charcoal and white, but without words, inspired a meaningful musical interpretation.

We followed the sounds of Africa everywhere her people were transported, especially to North America, the Caribbean, and Latin America. Students learned to copy rhythms unique to each style and accompany the music with small percussion and drums. They were willing to sing whenever the melodic content was catchy and easy to learn. Some of our most successful activities centered on songs from *Putumayo Presents, World Playground*: "Fatou Yo" (I am Fatou) from Senegal, "La Mariposa" (The Butterfly) from Bolivia, and "Three Little Birds" from Jamaica. Together with folk songs, they learned composed songs by Ladysmith Black Mambazo, "The Lion Song," Miriam Makeba, "The Click Song," and Taj Mahal, "Banana Boat Song."

That year we listened, sang, played instruments, and danced to music infused and inspired by the rhythms, modes, and stories of Africa. We learned about the origins of jazz and why New Orleans is known as the birthplace: that the first-wave jazz came from roots in African music intermingled with classical music of nineteenth-century France. People of many cultures migrated to New Orleans, including the Spanish, French,

African, Creole from Haiti, and Cajun from French Canada. Each nationality encountered the rhythms of others' languages, their songs, and the instruments they brought with them or found there. Cajuns played the concertina, accordion, and fiddle; and Africans created rhythm makers out of natural materials such as wood, rock, metal, animal bones, and skins. Students were grossed out (in a good way) when they learned that an instrument called the "jawbone" was made from the actual dried jawbone of a donkey, horse, or zebra. I demonstrated how the player uses his or her hands or sticks to scrape and tap out rhythms; and explained that the first players created this new sound from the buzzing sound made from the loosened teeth on the dried jawbone. We play a modern instrument that makes a buzzing sound that imitates the teeth-rattling of the jawbone—the vibra-slap. The vibra-slap was a big hit, and we added it to our increasing assortment of percussion voices. When I asked, "Did you know that the best-known instrument out of Africa is the banjo?" A chorus of protest went up from the class: "No way!" The students associated the banjo with country music—for white people. They, at first, refused to believe that black people ever played the banjo; and they were certain Africans did not invent it.

Children's enculturation begins early. All acquire attitudes, values, and behaviors expressed by their peers, families, and communities. Children in this all-black school didn't want to hear country music or opera. Rather than impose a generic repertoire, I selected music that engaged their attention. They responded to music of African cultures and to inspiring, majestic instrumental interpretations of patriotic anthems and military songs. Many students liked music that tells a story and popular songs from children's movies. They were amused at "old" rap music by M. C. Hammer and LL Cool J and a cover by Mickey Mouse of 1970s rap hits, all before rap went gangsta.

We explored the music and musicians of New Orleans's second-wave jazz when creativity and virtuosity of that city's musicians surpassed that of almost all artists who came before. We followed the routes of jazz up the Mississippi River to Memphis and Chicago. We traced the Delta Blues with Robert Johnson at the Crossroad, and B. B. King's Blues on Beale Street. We learned how Fats Domino and Little Richard took rhythm and blues all the way to Chuck Berry to Elvis and rock 'n' roll.

FINDING *YOUR* WAY

If students are not engaged in music that's meaningful to them, lessons fail; but when music and music-making activities are within their range of interest, abilities, and acceptability, students *are* motivated and willing to participate. Maintaining balance between music content and music activity is mercurial; you never know from one day to the next what will work. The best results come from compassion for students and systematic observations of classroom behavior, theirs and yours. As students become more engaged musically and willing to work together and with you, they will accept new repertoire and ways of making music.

You may find, as in Vivian Paley's example, that keeping a journal yields insights and supports reflection on your teaching and students' learning. As you write to yourself, the day's work comes into view and you can see the problems you need to solve, changes you need to make, and successes you can rely on. Questions worth asking and writing about: How interesting was the lesson content? Were there a variety of activities and learning experiences? Was the pace of the lesson managed effectively? Were my responses appropriate to the temperament and attentiveness of individual students? Do I show respect for all? Do I show that I care for each one?

My experience brings me to conclude that you cannot rely on premade curriculum and scripted music lessons planned by anyone else but you for the children you teach. Your ideas and the music you know are always the best possible curriculum. Children will help you learn the rest of what you need to know: how to understand and relate to them, plan for them, and teach them.

After a year in one school, especially if you keep a journal, you will have acquired greater knowledge of yourself and enhanced understanding of students and their abilities, attributes, and attitudes. You will know how to set the environment, customize the curriculum, find meaningful experiences that motivate your students, and make music learning and teaching successful, satisfying, and enjoyable. Creative teaching rests on these precepts; and it thrives in classrooms where flexibility, improvisation, and ingenuity are not constrained by relentless testing and mind-numbing standardization.

POSTSCRIPT

I was not rehired at the village school. A new principal came along . . . She wanted her "own people." I left feeling disappointed that my work was unfinished. I had much more to learn, ways to improve, and become a better teacher of the students I'd come to know and care about. The principal phoned me two months after the start of school: "I lost my music teacher. Will you come back?" By then, I was under contract for another position.[13]

NOTES

1. Coincidentally, both Arthur Rubinstein and Albert Einstein were delayed speakers.

2. She invites us to see, feel, and taste the roundness of "moon" and the grape from her grandpa's vine in Ohio. If told as a story on *Sesame Street*, they would add: *Brought to you by the letter O.*

3. Mary Chapin Carpenter, "Halley Came to Jackson," (https://youtu.be/Om3j8VP1oCI).

4. Peter Ustinov, *Dear Me*. Boston: Little, Brown, 1977.

5. Henri J. M. Nouwen, *Reaching Out: The Three Movements of the Spiritual Life*. Garden City, NY: Doubleday, 1975.

6. Mariah Carey, "Hero," (https://youtu.be/0IA3ZvCkRkQ).

7. *New York Times*, January 8, 1948, "Alfred North Whitehead: Evaluation of His Influence Presented by Supreme Court Justice," by Justice Felix Frankfurter.

8. James Garbarino, "An Ecological Perspective on the Role of Play in Child Development." In M. Block and A. Pellegrini (eds.), *The Ecological Context of Children's Play*. Norwood, NJ: Ablex, 1969.

9. The origin of the popular saying is unknown; however, the meaning is found in many African and American Indian proverbs and stories: "One hand cannot raise a child," and "A child does not grow up in a single home."

10. "Knowing yourself is the beginning of all wisdom." —Aristotle (384–322 BC) (www.biography.com/people/aristotle-9188415).

11. Lyrics to the song "Love Walked In" by George Gershwin.

12. Important caveat: This is not to say that children of color require a different education. Rather, I mean to show how customizing the delivery of instruction benefits student learning, honors their heritage, and provides a bridge to a comprehensive education in music and music making. This approach benefits all children.

13. My next school was wonderful, and I taught there for many years. When my students learned that I was unable to return the following year, they were as distressed as I: "What?" "You can't leave! You are our only hope!" "Will you come back when you feel better?" "Maybe you can come back as a substitute?"

FOUR

Inventiveness

Making Meaningful Music with Children

Only the best is good enough for children.
—Zoltán Kodály

There is music in children. Even very young children perceive the expressive qualities that give music meaning long before they acquire a lexicon of musical characteristics. Children know music from the inside; but if we teach music from the outside, without knowledge of children's experience of music, we lose our greatest resource for significant music teaching. Formalized pretesting, testing, and posttesting only get in the way of what we most want to know about the children we teach and the musical choices we make on their behalf.

This chapter concerns musicality as the essence of music learning and teaching and it examines the conditions of meaningful music making with children. Embedded throughout the essay are references to foundational influences in art, aesthetics, music, and education that are crucial to curriculum decisions and instructional actions: Herbert Read, *Education through Art* (1954); John Dewey, *Art as Experience* (1934); Alfred North Whitehead, *The Aims of Education* (1929), *Science and the Modern World* (1926); Susanne Langer, *Philosophy in a New Key* (1942), *Feeling and Form: A Theory of Art* (1953); Aaron Copland, *What to Listen For in Music* (1939); Leonard Bernstein, *The Joy of Music* (1959); Bennett Reimer, *A Philosophy of Music Education* (1970); Elliot Eisner, *The Arts and the Creation of Mind* (2002); and Jerome Bruner, *Toward a Theory of Instruction* (1966).

Each of these works is valued for its profound contribution toward understanding music as art and why this knowledge is important to teachers of children, especially children. That music's meaning embodies and flows from music's expressive qualities must prescribe each teacher's purpose for instruction. We know what to teach and how; however *why* we teach is fundamental to our orientation concerning music and children.

In the above-referenced book, American philosopher of mind and art Susanne Langer's new key refers to symbols of ideas and thoughts that go beyond what could be expressed in language. She wrote, "The real power of music lies in the fact that it can be true to the life of feeling in a way that language cannot; for its significant forms have that ambivalence of content that words cannot have" (p. 206).

Leonard Bernstein said it this way, "Music of all the arts, stands in a special region, unlit by any star but its own, and utterly without meaning . . . except its own." Bernstein and his mentor Aaron Copland engaged each other in conversations about music and the making of it for over forty years. Each musician spoke profusely about music through books, lectures, and personal letters. Consider Copland's advice in *What to Listen For in Music*:

> Whether you listen to Mozart or Duke Ellington, you can deepen your understanding of music only by being a more conscious and aware listener—not someone who is just listening, but someone who is listening for something. (p. 13)

Later in this popular little volume, Copland draws our attention to the formative quality of musical experience with or without the added value of professional study. Supplemental to this point, music education philosopher Bennett Reimer differentiates musical apprehension, that is, conceptual knowledge, *knowing about music*, with affective and perceptual knowledge, *knowing of music*. He offers a straightforward explanation of this distinction:

> In all cases, then, a concept is a mechanism by which one can refer to a noticed phenomenon. A concept is always about the phenomenon. It does not constitute the phenomenon itself or the internal experience of the phenomenon. A child may be taught that all things with certain qualities are called apples, and she may get the concept perfectly. But the experience of an apple when she eats it is of a different order. The concept is about the apple. The eating is of the apple. (p. 83)

Herbert Read, English poet, art historian, and critic, is wellknown for his influential works on the role of art in education. In *Education through Art*, he writes that the purpose of education is engagement in the intellectual and expressive processes of art:

> Education may therefore be defined as the cultivation of expression—it is teaching children and adults how to make sounds, images, movements, tools and utensils.
>   . . . All faculties of thought, logic, memory, sensibility and intellect are involved in such processes. And they are all processes which involve art, for art is nothing but the good making of sounds, images, etc.

The aim of education is therefore the creation of artists—of people efficient in various modes of expression. (p. 10)

Why are such theories of aesthetics, art, music, teaching, and learning necessary? Because we need to learn what the great thinkers have to say about the complexities of the nature of knowledge, the nature of the learner, and of the learning and developmental processes in order to construct, structure, and sequence curriculum. On this topic, American psychologist Jerome Bruner's work is authoritative.

In *Toward a Theory of Instruction*, Bruner makes the case for the differences between theories of learning and development and a theory of instruction, while explaining paradoxically how they are entwined. He explains that theories of learning and development derived from psychology are descriptive, whereas, a theory of instruction is prescriptive. "A theory of instruction, in short, is concerned with how what one wishes to teach can best be learned, with improving rather than describing learning" (p. 40). Furthermore, he contends that such a theory must be "congruent with those theories of learning and development to which it subscribes" (p. 40). Bruner proposes four major features of an instructional theory with implications for curriculum. These pertain to ecological conditions and relationships, structure of knowledge, and sequence and pacing of instruction.

Bruner asserts that any body of knowledge is relative, not absolute, given the child's ability and willingness to learn and the child's circumstances and gifts. The "establishment of knowledge" means teaching the child to participate in his or her own process of learning—"to get a student to think mathematically [or musically] for himself, to consider matters as an historian [and musician] does, to take part in the process of knowledge-getting. Knowledge is a process, not a product" (p. 72).

Neither is curriculum a product. John Goodlad, a preeminent educator, authored more than thirty important books on public education and democracy, teaching, and teacher education. He studied the results of curriculum with reference to student perceptions of what they had been taught. He found that what students acquire, the "experienced curriculum," differs from their experience of the "taught curriculum." That is, the taught curriculum, prescribed by and tested by external standards, tells more about what children do not know than what they do know or what they experience and understand. Consequently, when instructional practices become increasingly fragmented, children experience bits and pieces of information rather than knowledge of a meaningful, larger whole.

When subjected to multiple-choice testing, the taught curriculum splinters even further. What do children remember when the test is over? Think about the educational message, or better yet, consider children's experience of high-stakes testing. Children realize, all too soon (as early as kindergarten), that the information being tested, the required time for preparation and taking tests, are valued over everything else, music and art, social studies and science, physical education, and especially recess.

There are serious educational liabilities at work when curriculum is limited and ready-made instruction lacks imagination. Children are taught to *know* things without *making* things, and human cognition is limited to words and numbers. Knowledge is personal. Knowledge is acquired through the senses and then applied, expressed, and used.

MUSICAL TEACHING

Music's meaning emanates from music's expressive qualities. It follows that musicality ought to be the essence of our teaching and children's learning. When is musicality not the essence of a music lesson? When classroom and studio activities fail to engage students in the aesthetic experience of music. Specifically, *how* we teach singing, playing instruments, listening to music, creating music, or reading music, determines students' meaningful discovery, experience, and knowledge of music.

To be clear, this is not to imply that the study of musical characteristics should be ignored, rather it suggests that music's attributes and components are the very means by which music is fully experienced. Nonetheless, without a guiding philosophy of aesthetics and education, the art of music and the art of teaching are undermined or impaired.

What are some conditions that undermine musical teaching? The first is when music is used to teach something other than music, or when music is carelessly used to justify claims that it "teaches" other subjects. Scholar and author on arts education Elliot Eisner warned against justifications other than what is distinctive, *sui generis*, about music. Music is a unique form of human expression without equivalent. Such nonmusical justifications are misleading; furthermore, as they diminish music's value and meaningfulness, they rob children of musical perception, understanding, and knowing. Contrary to common banter, music is *not* a science, nor mathematical, a foreign language, or physical education. Nonmusical references distract from rather than support musical understanding. Decisions concerning music teaching demand attention to knowledge *of* and knowledge *about* music acquired only through realizing philosophical principles of aesthetic education. Otherwise, without a guiding philosophy, the very foundation and direction of learning are compromised.

The second condition that limits children's experience of music is when their "experienced curriculum" is limited to a singular system of thought, method, or approach. As we teach, we must ask if our work invites meaning making. For no matter the activity, if musicality is absent, meaning is lost. For example, while teaching by rote is an effective tool, if overused, students are denied opportunities to move and play instruments freely, to improvise, vocalize, and compose.

In other ways, children's musical knowing may be limited by too many memorized performances that take time away from classroom learning. Furthermore, consider whether playing musical games are more *game specific* than *musically valid*. You can easily tell the difference. If you hear more noise than music, the game would be better played at recess or in a physical education class. Or if children do not respond to or demonstrate musical behaviors, the game does not fit the definition of music learning.

The justification for teaching music must be based on music, not methodology. This is not to denigrate systematic methods, but rather to uphold a rich, varied, and meaningful experience of music whatever strategies are involved. Whitehead amuses with his witty remark on wrongminded teaching: "In the Garden of Eden, Adam saw the animals before he named them: in the traditional [educational] system, children name the animals before they saw them" (*Science and the Modern World*, p. 177).

Methodology over musicality prevails when music learning is standardized and subjected to nonmusical assessment. Musical culture and musical style always matter when teaching or performing music. Expressivity, meaning, and revelation must not yield to methodology. Teaching methods and strategies are the means to musical development, not the final goal. The delivery system is not the curriculum.

A third condition that interferes with students' full experience of music ensues when music's constituent parts artificially dissect a musical whole. Instruction formulated by this approach is uniquely structured toward teaching musical concepts one at a time. The prevailing idea suggests that if students focus on just one concept in a prescribed sequential order, they will have learned that concept and be prepared to move on to the next one. However, once the music comes apart—as experienced by children in this way—how will teachers put the music together again? (A Humpty Dumpty situation.) The disadvantage here follows as before: If the arbitrary dissection of musical concepts fails to embrace the intrinsic experience of music, then the method fails.

In *Feeling and Form*, Susanne Langer was explicit about "meaning making" when she wrote, "Elements with fixed and stable meanings cannot be comprehended by progressively building up an understanding of its parts in isolation. It must be understood as a whole." Music is experienced as a temporal phenomenon, and unlike the literary and visual arts, music is apprehended all parts at once—*gleich alles zusammen*, to quote Mozart.

Contrived systems of pedagogy may be misapplied in the music studio, the classroom, or across cultures. Implementation of unvarying, systematic, standardized procedures distorts understanding and may result in teacher boredom and student indifference. Imitation techniques are generally successful; but when children continually copy their teacher's actions of patterned movement and vocalizations, creative music learning ceases to thrive. On a much larger scale, when the outstandingly successful *El Sistema* was transferred from Venezuela to Scotland, critics there questioned the efficacy of its publicly financed goals of social change through music compared with "the more individualist society of contemporary Britain." As Stephanie Pitts, in *Chances and Choices: Exploring the Impact of Music Education*, reasons, "Cultural and educational sensibilities in different countries might mean that a transfer of ideals, rather than methods, should be the focus of such a campaign" (p. 172).

MUSICAL AUTHENTICITY

The integrity of a musical education is determined by the excellence of music children sing, listen to, and by the quality of instruments they play. Given the scarcity of funds for musical resources, instruments, and equipment, too often teachers must decide on what is affordable over what is preferable. Even so, choices concerning practicality must yield to the aims of musicality. Only music that is stylistically authentic (performers and performances, instruments and instrumentation) is good enough for teaching and learning music of any given style, whether, American jazz and folk music, European, Latin, Asian art music, traditional world music, or commercial popular music.

MUSICAL REPERTOIRE[1]

Authenticity is important as each teacher collects and builds her own music repertoire of songs and scores, recordings, and videos. A nonscientific scroll through Amazon's list of the most popular music for children reveals kid-friendly mixes and covers of current pop and rap performers. The apparent purpose of these recordings is to give younger kids a cleaner version of songs they like (or that older siblings like). Sort of like *youngsta* versus *gangsta*. Parent reviewers on Amazon said they disliked their kid-friendly music purchases because the lyrics and the messages conveyed were inappropriate and the music garbage. Another parent commented, "It's irritating, but kids love it." The kid voices and instrumental tracks on the CDs I listened to were mostly loud and repetitive, and not in a good way.

Children and adults are sure to love music for kids if the songs are great, the singers and instrumentalists are first rate, and the styles are captivating. Some of my favorites for K–5 students are by Sandra Boynton and Michael Ford, *Frog Trouble and Eleven Other Pretty Serious Songs* (2013); *Maurice Ravel, Bolero Completely Unraveled for Orchestra and Kazoos* (2010); *Blue Moo: 17 Jukebox Hits from Way Back Never* (2008); *Dog Train: A Wild Ride on the Rock and Roll Side* (2005); *Rhinoceros Tap: 15 Seriously Silly*

Songs (2004); *Philadelphia Chickens* (2002); *Grunt: Pigorian Chant from Snou-to Domoniko Silo* (1996). Each audio CD comes with a cleverly illustrated book, including song lyrics and scores for easy accompaniment. Boynton and Ford attract and hold children's and teachers' attention through songs that are at once musical and mischievous.

For a delightful introduction to this music, go to YouTube: *Sandra Boynton's Behind the Moosic: The Making of Blue Moo.* Boynton shows how this popular album evolved into original compositions and performances of the "optimistic, energetic, and magical" 1950s jukebox music. Christopher Kale Jones, who portrayed Frankie Valli in *Jersey Boys*, performs "Singing in the Shower"; Sha Na Na sing variations on the word *banana* in the "Gorilla Song"; Steve Lawrence croons "Blue Moo," about a singing cow; Brian Wilson recreated that famous sound and hot-rod theme from "Little Deuce Coup" in "Speed Turtle"; Neil Sedaka's style comes through "Your Nose"; B. B. King's solo "One Shoe Blues" is a simple, classic, blues-singing-playing-teaching song; Patti LuPone sings "Rabbit Tango," for real. You'll hear Davy Jones, Gerry and the Pacemakers, and cocreator Michael Ford & the Uninvited Loud Precision Band, Darcy Boynton, Keith Boynton, and Devin McEwan.

Let me tell you a story from my classroom about "Rabbit Tango," sung by Patti LuPone. To begin, do you recognize this fifth-grade student? He's very funny and disruptive, and he's always starting something. One day, as the students and I were playing Latin percussion with this tongue-in-cheek Tango, this one started goofing off again. [*Note to self: Don't scold—surprise!*] As the music played, I gestured with dramatic intent and invited my rascally student to come to the front of the class. To *his* surprise, I held out my hand; to *my* surprise, he took it and followed my lead in an over-the-top ersatz tango. The class applauded as we danced back and forth and back and forth across the room. It was fantastic; one of those spontaneous, unplanned, unforgettable, teaching experiences savored by teachers like me. From that day on Tango Boy was an asset, not an agitation.

Such delightful songs are music-teaching gems. "Singing in the Shower" from *Blue Moo*, proved as popular with fifth graders as kindergarten students. The refrain is immediately singable, the verses are hilarious, and the singer and instrumentation is pure Frankie Valli. Check it out on YouTube:[2]

> *Singing in the shower!*
> *Singing in the shower!*
> *Singing in the shower!*
> *I'm singing in the shower again!*

Every morning when I wake up,
well, my voice is all wrong. You can
hardly even hear me sing my song.
But I step into the shower,
there's a whole new sound
as soon as the water's coming down.

On to Carnegie Hall, "and you know I'll be bringing my own shower stall" wearing "waterproof tuxedos, maybe purple satin Speedos."

Students learned the lyrics quickly as they pantomimed moves like washing hair and scrubbing up and down and all around. (What is so funny about armpits?) Some wanted maracas, claves, or whatever, for microphones. Isn't it magic when students are fully motivated by the music and they really want to sing, play instruments, move, dance, pantomime, and improvise? Wait, wait . . . you want to know, what's the objective? Any and all of the following:

1. Performing: Singing on pitch, in rhythm, with appropriate dynamics, timbre, and steady tempo.
2. Performing: Playing instruments in groups, blending instrumental timbres and dynamic levels, and/or playing independent instrumental parts while other students sing or play contrasting parts.
3. Improvising: Make up movements in response to the musical style, improvise rhythmic variations in the music's style.
4. Symbolizing and reading: Use a system (solfeggio) to read simple pitch patterns (treble clef) from the song (short, repetitive patterns "singing in the shower").
5. Symbolizing and writing: Identify dynamic, tempo, and stylistic articulation features throughout the recorded performance; create a visual representation and apply traditional markings for expressive qualities.

Depending on the musical and developmental needs of the students you teach, you are encouraged to target more than one of these objectives within a single lesson or over many lessons. When students exclaim, "Let's do it again," you have a favorable chance to reinforce the current objectives and/or introduce new skills and concepts. This is your recipe for success: *Follow the music and the children will follow you.*

Few children in my school knew Mister Rogers, much less his songs, but when they were introduced to *Songs from the Neighborhood: The Music of Mister Rogers* (2005) students responded, as did their parents' generation, to Fred Rogers's nurturing, imaginative, and you-are-special songs: "Won't You Be My Neighbor" is performed by Jon Secada and again by Roberta Flack; Amy Grant sings "It's You I Like"; B. J. Thomas performs "It's Such a Good Feeling"; CeCe Winans does "Then Your Heart Is Full of Love"; John Pizzarelli sings "What Do You Do?"; Maureen McGovern performs "This Is Just the Day"; Toni Rose sings "Just for Once"; Ricky Skaggs does "Let's Think of Something to Do While We're Waiting"; and Donna Summer sings "Are You Brave?"

MUSICAL INSTRUMENTS

The principles of authenticity apply to all musical instruments children play. Bucket drums, no matter how convenient and plentiful, cannot replace the rich resonance of djembes, bongos, congas, tom-toms, *tubanos*, timbales, and hand drums. Children are alert to the tone color of all instruments they play, whether drums or small percussion, the vibra-slap, guiro, *shekeres*, tambourines, triangles, and cowbells. Given their increasing understanding of *timbre*, students are eager to learn best practices of playing in style, musical style, that is.

A Music Lesson Plan Format

Title_____

Date_____

Grade Level_____

Musical Skills	**Content Standards**
1. Listening	A. Musical Skills
2. Singing	B. Creativity
3. Playing Instruments	C. Culture/History
4. Moving/Dance	D. Analysis
5. Improvising	E. Life Experience
7. Creating	F. Evaluation
8. Symbolizing/Reading	G. Assessment

IDEAS, PROCEDURES, AND MATERIALS FOR INSTRUCTION

Shiver Me Timbres![3]

Objective: Students will discern differences in *timbre* (tone color) quality between selected percussion instruments through listening and playing instruments.

Introduction and Warm-up:

a. Invite students to listen to and compare the sound quality of rhythm sticks and the claves (A, 1). Refers to format above. (A) Musical Skills (1) Listening.

b. Ask two students to demonstrate improvise rhythms, talk back and forth. (A) Musical Skills (3) Playing Instruments.

Procedures:

c. *Let's play a listening game.*

This listening activity can be played with any two instruments to discern differences in *timbre* quality.

The game begins:

> *Close your eyes.*
> *Listen to the sound of thing One.*
> *Don't look yet.*
> *Now, listen to thing Two.*
> *Open your eyes.*
> *What did you hear?*
> *How is thing One different from thing Two?*

After a few goofy answers, "It's a bird . . . it's a plane." "No, it's Woody Woodpecker," the fourth graders responded with perceptive comparisons about the musical quality of each instrument. We compared differences in instruments and discussed *timbre*: why the sound quality of instruments is important in music and how even different playing techniques can alter the sound of the instrument. (A, 1) Musical Skills-Listening, (C, 1) Cultural/Historical Contexts-Listening, (F) Evaluation-Observation.

d. The teacher explains: *Professional percussion players play this instrument. It looks like two fat sticks, but these are made of rosewood due to the musical resonance this special wood produces. The difference between playing claves like two fat sticks or playing them as an authentic instrument is well . . . striking.*

Listen, this way, you get a flat, dull sound. Playing like a pro is more complicated, but the sound is really exciting. Try it like this: Hold one of the claves in your left (or nondominant) hand. Make a hollow space by curving your fingers and thumb as a resting place for the clave. Don't squeeze. Just let it sit on top of your fingers. With the other hand, hold the clave lightly and tap it with the other one. Position them so that the center of each strikes the other. Experiment to find the sweet spot where the sound is best. You can switch one for the other and get a different sound . . . like this. (A, 3) Musical Skills, Playing Instruments, (D, 1, 3) Analysis, Playing Instruments, Listening.

e. Very few sets of claves are needed among the other percussion you might have in your classroom because their sound penetrates and adds a high sonority heard sharply over all other instruments. With two sets, you can exchange rhythms with a student or invite two students to play together in a rhythmic call and response. (A, 3) Musical Skills, Playing Instruments, (B, 3, 5) Creating, Playing Instruments, Improvising.

f. Children's experience of music is enriched when teachers use story-telling infused with memorable facts in responses to questions like "Where'd that come from?" and "Who made it?" (C, 1) Cultural/Historical Contexts-Listening. The following background supports this lesson:

Claves originated in the hardwood forests of Cuba where Spanish conquistadores discovered rosewood, a unique wood for shipbuilding. African slaves, who built the Spanish ships, gathered leftover planks and the discarded wooden pegs for their own use, most especially, making music instruments. Forbidden to make drums by their Spanish masters, slaves used the sharp, resonant sound of the hardwood to create the first known claves model. This newfound sound source gave these indentured laborers another means to express their musical heritage born in Mother Africa — and the sound traveled with them throughout North and South America and beyond. (C) Culture/History.

g. To expand students' experiences of African and Latin percussion, we listened and moved to selected Afro-Cuban music. The lively rhythms always captured children's interest in playing claves and other indigenous Afro-Latin, Afro-Caribbean percussion, and in creating spontaneous and practiced dance moves. They particularly liked the music on the CD *Cuba* by Putumayo World Music. Each selection has a strong presence of claves and exciting rhythms that students could easily identify and imitate, or freely improvise.

h. *Fiesta* by the Simón Bolívar Youth Orchestra of Venezuela with Gustavo Dudamel is another exciting recording of Latin music styles. The claves are prominent in Arturo Márquez, "Danzón No. 2" (Mexico); and Leonard Bernstein's "Mambo" from *West Side Story*.
(A, 1, 3, 4, 5) (B, 3, 4, 5) (C, 1, 3) (D, 1, 3, 4) (F, 1, 3, 4, 5) (F)

i. The voice is often overlooked in lessons on timbre. In this lesson, students listen and compare differences in voices and sing in style. Two songs cited previously are appropriate here: "Fatou yo" from *World Playground* (Putumayo). "I am Fatou," sung in Mandingo, is from Senegal. The language is fascinating and children find it easy and fun to sing. The second, "Three Little Birds," is a cheerful reggae song: "Every little thing is gonna be all right." "Bongo Bong," a song with irresistible rhythm, is about a little monkey who loves to play the bongo whether anyone likes it or not. *Latin Playground* by Putumayo presents "Guantanamera" with children singing the refrain; *Cielito Lindo* entices students to sing, play instruments, and improvise Afro-Latin moves (A, 1, 2, 3, 4, 5).

Let's play. Now you are a part of this performance.
Pay attention, we must keep time with them since they cannot follow us.

Based on musical themes, the following plans yield enough content for several lessons and adaptations for students in kindergarten through grade five. In your search for materials, keep relevant background notes, teaching ideas, and repertoire in a digital file for future reference. Planning in this way adds depth to your knowledge of music's historical and cultural contexts within a comprehensive repertoire of musical compositions. There is added value to such detailed planning, especially when you are being reviewed and evaluated. The next plan follows the rubrics for elementary school social studies.

IDEAS, PROCEDURES, AND MATERIALS FOR INSTRUCTION

American Indian Legends, Songs, Drums, and Dances: Dancing Drums and Singing Clay

Student Target:

I [student] can explain and demonstrate how American Indians used legends, songs, drums, and dances to communicate and express beliefs about their world. Note: I am intentionally using the term American Indian rather than Native American. In a 1995 U.S. census, most native peoples preferred *American Indian* to *Native American*. In 2004 a new museum opened on the Mall in Washington and selected the traditional title, National Museum of the American Indian.

Equipment: Computer, LCD projector and screen; audio CD player

Musical instruments: American Indian drums, rattles, bells, flute

Books for Children: *When Clay Sings; American Indian Legends, Dancing Drum—A Cherokee Legend; Turquoise Boy—A Navajo Legend; Quillworker—A Cheyenne Legend; Legend of the Bluebonnet; Giving Thanks—A Native American Good Morning Message*

Books for Teachers: *A Cry from the Earth: Music of the North American Indians; Keepers of the Fire: Journey to the Tree of Life*, based on Black Elk's Vision; *Keepers of the Animals: American Indian Stories and Wildlife Activities for Children; Visions of a Vanishing Race: Photographs by Edward Sheriff Curtis*

Audio CDs: *Earth Spirit* by R. Carlos Nakai, Native American flute solo; *Squanto and the First Thanksgiving*, Graham Greene, storyteller, Paul McCandless, music; *Smithsonian Folkways: Music of the Plains Indians; A*

Cry from the Earth: Music of North American Indians; Music in the Time of Columbus: Iberian Composers; Home for the Harvest: Music for Thanksgiving.

DVD: *Into the Circle: An Introduction to the Powwow*

Procedures:

Warm-up: Imagine the first sightings of Europeans by American Indians. What might they have observed about these strangers? Display images for points of discussion. What might the Europeans have observed about the American Indians? Invite students to describe American Indians and Europeans in their earliest encounters.

Instruct students to reject any assumptions that cannot be validated by historical accounts. What is known about the language, culture, music, and past generations of each? Artifacts and legends, and eyewitness accounts. Show students what we know from authentic documentation, first-person accounts, and from legends and past memories. Compare and contrast means of recording history by the Europeans and the American Indians: oral tradition, written tradition.

1. Invite students to explore music of the American Indian: Play selected segments of *Earth Spirit* by R. Carlos Nakai. Ask students: Describe the material used in making this flute. What do you think the song—without words—means? That is, what is the player expressing through the song? Celebration? Healing? Grief?
2. Guide students in a dance-movement realization of selected solos by Nakai. Guide students to discover musical structure and phrases, melodic direction, and expressivity.
3. Provide American Indian instruments and direct students in creating characteristic music. Suggest: How would celebration music sound? How would sad music sound? American Indians recreated the music and dance of their ancestors. Let's play music that might sound like theirs. What instruments do we need? Describe the traditional dress of different American Indians: Plains Indians, Cherokee, and Seminole. Create a checklist of student assumptions about differences among these three nations. View *Into the Circle* DVD to validate or challenge assumptions.
4. Explore American Indian legends and beliefs about their world. Present one of the children's books on legends of the Cherokee, Navajo, or Cheyenne. Use pull-down maps to indicate migration and location of selected tribes and nations. Ask students to surmise how each shared their collective knowledge to explain their world view: movements of the moon, cycle of seasons, planting and growing, cycles of life and death, peace and war, gifts of wisdom of animals, the spirit and guidance of ancestors, reverence for Mother Earth and her life-giving powers.

5. Display text of American Indian poetry. Invite students to read aloud. Identify and analyze poetry for expressive meaning, poetic images and content, and beliefs about the Earth's ecology and reverence for life for all that is living and life-giving. Ask students to select a poem and translate its meaning in their own words.

6. Listen to *Music in the Time of Columbus: Iberian Composers*. Compare and contrast language, vocal and instrumental music, culture and style of living. What might the music of American Indians and Europeans have in common? What are the meaningful differences among them?

7. What do American Indians believe about the world, the environment, community, ancestors, and future of the planet? Compare your beliefs about ecology. Saving the planet. Resources of air, water, earth, animals, and people.

8. Vocabulary: Native American, American Indian, legend, artifacts, eyewitness, oral tradition, indigenous peoples, European colonization, assimilation, resistance, removal, Navajo, Cherokee, Seminole, and Cheyenne.

ESOL Strategies:

Language Learning Activities
1. Concentration Game
Prepare pockets: A – B – C – D – E and numbers.
Select vocabulary terms and create matching pairs.
Provide definitions on back of cards.
Divide students by groups.
Explain game rules and point system.
Model game, monitor game, review vocabulary.

2. Listen, Identify, Analyze
Provide students sets of index cards for each of the selected topics. On each card include descriptive words and/or vocabulary about: American Indian legends, music, or customs as indicated. Ask students to listen to each musical example and select the vocabulary cards that best describes the music.

3. Oral Presentation
Arrange the students into groups according to topics selected. Give students a time limit to share and discuss their card choices. Guide them to collaborate and present their collective ideas and findings to the class.

Assessments:

a. Students will be assessed on cross checklists concerning lesson content.

b. Students will be evaluated on contributions to discussion topics.

c. Students will be evaluated on musical performances as directed. Ask students to demonstrate rhythmic skills and drumming techniques with selected musical examples.

d. Students will be assessed on factual information, map skills, and vocabulary.

e. Students will be evaluated on understanding of American Indian culture.

f. Students will be assessed on their answers to short essay questions on American Indian legends.

Wrap-up:

Guide students in developing a multimedia presentation of main points and features of American Indian legends, songs, drums, and dances.

Enrichment:

Organize an American Indian Festival Day throughout the school. Provide interested teachers, staff, and parent volunteers with materials and guidelines to create displays, dramas, costume parades, food events, and music. Record episodes and create a DVD to share with family and friends.

Standards-Benchmarks for Social Studies:

S.S. 5. A. 1. 1. Using primary and secondary sources to understand history.

S.S. 5. A. 1. 2. Use timelines to identify and discuss American history time periods.

S.S. 5. A. 3. 2. Investigate European explorers.

S.S. 5. A. 3. 2. Describe interactions among American Indians and Europeans.

IDEAS, PROCEDURES, AND MATERIALS FOR INSTRUCTION

American Composer George Gershwin: A Jazzy Classic
Got Rhythm?

Student Target:

Discover George Gershwin; perform jazz rhythms in the style of Gershwin on percussion instruments; examine Gershwin's musical contributions in jazz and classical styles; and understand the cultural and historical contexts of Gershwin's place of importance in the Jazz Age.

Equipment: Computer, LCD projector and screen, audio CD player

Books for Children: *Rhapsody in Blue* with CD; Gershwin: *American Rhapsody* with CD

DVD: *Fantasia: Rhapsody in Blue*—Disney animation

Film Clip: *American in Paris:* "I Got Rhythm"—Gene Kelly and children

Websites: www.gershwin.org; www.jalc.org (Jazz at Lincoln Center); www.pbs.org/fromthetop (Jazz performances by students)

Audio CDs: Selections for orchestra, piano, and jazz band; *Rhapsody in Blue*; Variations on "I Got Rhythm"; *An American in Paris*; "Cuban Overture"; "Fascinating Rhythm"; "Walking the Dog"; "Strike up the Band"; Medley from *Porgy and Bess*

Musical Instruments: Rhythmic percussion, bongo and conga drums, claves, maracas, temple blocks, vibra-slap, cabasa

Whiteboard Display: Rhythmic notation from selected Gershwin songs and compositions

Procedures:
   Warm-up: Play a brief excerpt of classical style, Mozart's Piano Concerto in E-flat Major, K. 271. In contrast, play Gershwin's *Rhapsody in Blue* and invite students to describe contrasts between the Mozart concerto and Gershwin's piano and orchestral composition.

Activities: Teaching and Learning Experiences
   a. Invite students to listen and describe a CD recording of Gershwin's *Rhapsody in Blue*. Guide students in discovering the jazz elements characteristic of this work.
   b. Show DVD: Disney's *Fantasia* animation of *Rhapsody in Blue*. Guide students in describing the relationship between Gershwin's music and the animation storyline with attention to repetition and contrast, part to whole, beginning-middle-end.
   c. Introduce Gershwin's life and times: son of Jewish immigrants; experienced jazz music; heard musicians play in his neighborhood; learned to play piano from his older brother, Ira's, piano lessons.
   d. Present Gershwin website www.gershwin.org to show the collaboration between George and Ira as they wrote music together for Broadway shows, Hollywood films, and numerous popular songs that became standards in the jazz repertoire.
   e. Play "Strike up the Band" and invite individual students to assume the role of conductor. Provide percussion instruments for students to play as accompaniment. Invite students to create a marching band with flags and simple marching drill patterns.

f. Introduce a film clip: *An American in Paris*, Gene Kelly performing "I Got Rhythm" as song and tap dance with a group of children. Follow with CD recording, *Variations on "I Got Rhythm."* Provide rhythmic percussion instruments for players in small groups.

g. Introduce first few bars of "Promenade" ("Walking the Dog"). Ask students to identify jazz elements: rhythm, melody, and ensemble. Demonstrate syncopated rhythms on temple blocks and direct individual students in improvisations based on syncopation patterns. Add contrasting percussion instruments: vibra-slap and cabasa for beat and accents. Show rhythmic patterns notation on whiteboard or prepared charts for music reading practice.

Wrap-up:

Return students' attention to www.gershwin.org. Review timeline highlights of Gershwin's life: early years influenced by jazz and trained in classical music; worked as a song plugger at age fifteen; became an accomplished pianist; collaborated with brother Ira as songwriters; prolific composer: Gershwin on Broadway, Gershwin in concert, and Gershwin on film. Jukebox and YouTube offer access to audio and video clips of Gershwin songs and compositions. Show students website link to the complete listing of Gershwin's music and to another link for downloading sheet music and scores.

Gershwin by the numbers: 9, 26, 1898, 15, 7, 11, 1937, 38: birthday 9, 26, 1898; first job as a song plugger at age 15; date when he died, 7, 11, 1937; he was 38 years old.

Vocabulary: percussion, idiophone, vibra-slap, cabasa, temple blocks, syncopation, blue notes, rhapsody, jazz style, classical style, Jazz Age, orchestra, jazz band, Broadway show, Jacob Gershowitz, Tin Pan Alley, song plugger.

Daily Assessments:

a. Students will be assessed on listening activities: "Name That Gershwin Tune."

b. Students will be assessed on completion of a quiz on The Life, Times, and Music of George Gershwin.

c. Students will be assessed on knowledge of relevant vocabulary: rhapsody, syncopation, blue notes, jazz and classical musical styles, composer, George Gershwin, lyricist, Ira Gershwin, the Jazz Age.

d. Students will be evaluated on rhythmic accuracy playing selected percussion instruments.

ESOL Strategies:
Language Learning Activities
   1. Concentration Game
   Prepare pockets: A – B – C – D – E and numbers.
   Select vocabulary terms and create matching pairs.
   Provide definition on back of cards.
   Divide students by groups.
   Explain game rules and point system.
   Model game, monitor game, review vocabulary.
   2. Listen, Identify, Analyze
   Provide students sets of index cards for each of the selected topics.
On each card include descriptive words and/or vocabulary. Ask students
to listen to each musical example and select the vocabulary cards that
best describe the music.
   3. Oral Presentation
   Arrange students into groups according to topics selected. Give
students a time limit to share and discuss their card choices. Guide them
to collaborate and present their collective ideas and findings to the class.

Standards-Benchmarks:
   MU.A (Musical Skills) 2.2 MU.B (Creativity) 2.2.2
   MU.C (Culture/History) 1.2.1
   MU.C. 1.2.4. MU. D (Analysis/Cognition) 1.2.1 MU.D.1.2.2
   MU.E. (Life Experience) 2.2.4

Enrichment:
   Create a Jazz Age performance, including dancers, singers, and percussion players with selected musical compositions by George Gershwin.

IDEAS, PROCEDURES, AND MATERIALS
FOR THEMATIC INSTRUCTION

Children love birthdays and the idea of birthdays. Celebrating a specific
composer's birthday each month excites interest and draws attention to
where and when each one lived. Children often ask, "What did he or she
die of?" "Are there any composers not dead?" If you are a good storyteller, students will remember the best tales about the composer and be able
to relate the most interesting facts with the music he or she wrote. These
are some of the composers and compositions I selected for Composer-of-
the-Month instruction:

August	Leonard Bernstein, *West Side Story*, "Mambo," "Cha-Cha-Cha"
September	George Gershwin, *Rhapsody in Blue*; "Strike up the Band"
October	Camille Saint-Saëns, *Carnival of the Animals*
November	Aaron Copland, *Billy the Kid*; *Appalachian Spring*
December	Ludwig van Beethoven, Symphony no. 5
January	Wolfgang Amadeus Mozart, *Eine kleine Nachtmusik*; *The Magic Flute*
February	George Frideric Handel, *Water Music*; *Music for the Royal Fireworks*
March	Johann Sebastian Bach, "Little" Fugue for Organ in G Minor; Air on a G String from Orchestral Suite no. 3 in D Major
April	Sergei Prokofiev, *Peter and the Wolf*; "Montagues and Capulets" from *Romeo and Juliet*; *Lieutenant Kije*
May	Pyotr Ilyich Tchaikovsky, *Swan Lake*; *1812 Overture*

In each month, I created an instructional theme as an organizational tool for music repertoire and learning experiences, singing, playing instruments, moving to music, improvising and composing music, and listening to and analyzing music. In this manner, teachers may make plans ahead and simplify the search for ideas and materials. These instructional themes are coordinated with Composers-of-the-Month corresponding cited above.

August	Around the World with Music
September	Sing Me an American Song
October	Animal Music
November	Roots and Branches of American Music
December	Instruments of the Orchestra
January	Mozart and His Music
February	Music in the Times of Kings and Presidents
March	Bach Is in the House
April	The Russians Are Coming
May	Music Tells a Story

MUSICAL EVALUATION AND ASSESSMENT[4]

There are pedagogical advantages when music teachers think about evaluation as the immediate, informal means of ascertaining students' performance and progress of musical skills. In all settings — rehearsal hall, classroom, and private lessons — musician-teachers continuously evaluate and provide immediate feedback that is at once succinct, specific, and timely. In the classroom or rehearsal setting, unique training and abilities of attention equip teachers, directors, and conductors to detect, solve musical problems, and evaluate music making by groups of students. However, when judged by non-musician administrators, these targeted musical skills and point-by-point evaluations of students' performances may go unnoticed or be misunderstood. For this reason, some music teachers feel anxious about being evaluated. This is one teacher's story: Following a thirty-minute classroom evaluation, the evaluator asked, "What is the point of this?" What the administrator failed to comprehend was the plurality of musical skills being taught and learned. She expected answers with a point coequal to a lesson activity on numeracy or literacy. Despite the written lesson plan with clearly defined musical objectives, content, and learning experiences that resulted in a successful lesson, the evaluator noted, "Nothing was finished . . . there were no achievable [measurable] results."

A word of encouragement to music teachers under such scrutiny — *use your words*. Identify and communicate what you teach with musical terms and concepts; do not give way to terminology that is ill fitting, inexact, and nonmusical. It takes diplomacy and firmness to get your point across that music education, knowing music and how to teach it, is your *métier*.

Pencil and paper tests are not as effective in the music classroom as the rehearsal techniques exclusive to music teaching and learning. However, systematic, measured, formal assessment can be meaningful with upper-elementary students. Lessons about the music of composers, their lives, and relevant cultural and historical contexts may be assessed in a variety of ways, including a short quiz, end of unit essay, or oral report, especially when documentation is required. More creative assessment ideas can be incorporated as learning experiences, for example, "What is one word that describes this music?" "What if . . . you play the music differently and/or on different instruments?" "Can you make a story from this music?" "How do you expect this music to end?" "What would you name this music?" "Could you make a drawing of this music?" Such open-ended questions apply to a music-listening activity, an improvisation with instruments or voices, and composition. Examinations of students' music-reading skills achieved through performance and dictation tasks, provide additional assessment tools for documentation and reporting.

As you might expect, even young students are more attentive if a test is involved. Their worry, "Is this on a test?" combined with test-exhaustion suggests that standardization and high-risk testing have contaminated students' conception of learning. Is it too late to unpollute the rivers of learning? Confirmation that children need music and greatly benefit from education in music has never been more evident than in the present era of Common Core Standards, frequent assessment, teacher liability, and curriculum restriction.

British composer and influential music educator John Paynter (2008) distinguishes the demands of music with academic endeavors:

> It will not suffice to impose on music a spurious academicism to make it appear rigorous in exactly the same terms as some other curriculum subjects. Apart from anything else that is unnecessary: music has its own rigour in the demands of sensitivity, imagination, and inventiveness common to all artistic endeavour—qualities which are sorely needed in the modern world. (p. 187)
>
> . . . In all of this work of poets, painters, musicians, sculptors, dancers—indeed every kind of creative artist—is crucial, principally because they all try to come to terms with what is sensed, what is felt, rather than with what is merely measured or calculated. (p. 192)

WHEN CHILDREN SING

Children are born to be singers. Infants coo and babble in song. Toddlers imitate what they hear and make up sounds and songs of their own. Some children sing themselves to sleep. Some make up songs wherever they are, riding in the car, bus, or subway train, going for a walk, taking a bath, playing with toys, or just waiting and waiting on someone. Pretend play invites children's singing; similarly, children's favorite songs encourage and lead them to invent fantasy play. There are "air guitarists" and "hairbrush divas" who like to perform on their own improvised wibbly-wobbly stage for imaginary or real audiences.

Teaching singing in the music classroom offers special opportunities and challenges. Take into consideration: (a) children's singing abilities and experience; (b) time and space available; (c) group singing; (d) musicals; (e) chorus; (f) styles of singing, traditional, classical, pop, and world music cultures; (g) repertoire and genres; (h) care and training of the young voice.

First, do no harm. . . . Have you noticed that over time many young singers with naturally beautiful voices have been encouraged to sing too much, too soon, too loud? In some instances, their perfectly positioned, clear child voice is lost and soon replaced by a more commercially appealing big sound. Many child prodigies seem to fade away as they get older. Perhaps some lost interest and some lost their voices. When little ballet dancers stand in *pointe* shoes too soon, their soft growing bones can be damaged, resulting in lasting harm. There must be an equivalent in gymnastics and other sports involving young children who are not yet physically developed for the tasks required.

At times, when students take untoward singing behaviors too far in seeking novelty, excitement, and funny stuff, it is time to raise the challenge level and insist on higher expectations. Such an opportunity unfolded in a singing lesson that began with the question, "Who knows the story of 'The Star-Spangled Banner'?"

Students knew about Francis Scott Key and his inspiration for the song. When I asked, "Who knows about the War of 1812 and Fort McHenry?" one boy said, "We went there last summer on vacation." Others discussed, guessed, surmised, and speculated about the song's origins. Briefly, I provided factual information that led students to understand and properly sing "The Star-Spangled-Banner." Together, we staged a drama with students in improvised roles as reporters circa 1812.

"Breaking News." "Reporting Live from Baltimore Harbor."
Reporters assumed positions on the coastline of the Chesapeake Bay. They described the star-shaped Fort McHenry and explained the military strategy that was involved when deciding on its particular construction. Reports ensued on the nautical position of the British ships and the twenty-five-hour bombardment of Fort McHenry. Bystanders recorded news flashes and mapped battleship positions on the newsroom white board.

"Pictures just in . . . Rockets streaming over the ramparts!"
Spies got word that the young lawyer, Frances Scott Key, watched the battle's fury while he was a prisoner aboard one of the British ships. *"What is he writing?"* shouted an onsite reporter, turned spy. Immediately, she sent the spy decoders to secure the document and decipher its meaning.

I can barely read it in the dim light. It says . . .
Oh, say, can you see by the dawn's early light

A crowd of townspeople and bystanders responds:
"What does this mean? What is he looking at?"

What so proudly we hailed at the twilight's last gleaming?

Crowd: What was it they "hailed" the night before the battle?
Who knows another code word for "hailed"?

Whose broad stripes and bright stars, thru the perilous fight,

Crowd: What broad stripes and bright stars . . . in the perilous fight?
Translate the message here.

O'er the ramparts we watched, were so gallantly streaming?

Crowd: What are ramparts? What do they mean by streaming?
I don't understand.

And the rockets' red glare, the bombs bursting in air,

Crowd: Rockets—who's firing rockets?

Gave proof through the night that our flag was still there.

Crowd: What proof? Whose flag was still "there"?
Reporter, "This looks like the end of the spy document! It says . . ."

*Oh, say does that Star-Spangled Banner yet wave
O'er the land of the free and the home of the brave?*

Crowd: "Star-Spangled Banner"—is this a code, a symbol? Explain!
Reporter: Stay calm and rescue Frances Scott Key!

Following our reenactment, I said, "Let's sing it." Without prompting, they stood up, listened for the introduction, and watched the cues from the piano. Now what? Some of the fourth-grade students started singing with loud, silly voices. Where did they get this bad idea? Hearing too many failed solo performances at sporting events on television? Even so, they knew that their preposterous singing was short-lived. I interceded as follows:

> First, you may not disrespect this song, or the American flag, or the Pledge of Allegiance. Second, you will practice good singing. That means, right notes, correct pitch and rhythm, phrasing and breath control, enunciation, vowels and consonants, entrances, cut-offs, head voice, not pop voice. Third, you will keep your eyes on the conductor—that would be me—at all times.

With expectations significantly raised and skills challenged, we worked our way through the musical difficulties the song presents. "Again! You can do better." They whined, "Can we sit down?" "I'm getting tired." and "*You* get to sit down—why can't we?" (What's with these tired old people?) Their efforts were encouraged and each accomplishment praised. "You could not have sung so well even a few minutes ago." By the end of the lesson-rehearsal, the students stood up straight, and sang "The Star-Spangled Banner" beautifully and musically. "Now that you know the background, purpose, and meaning of our national anthem, sing it in your best voice with the pride of patriotism," and they did each time from then on. When their teacher came to pick them up for lunch, they asked, "Please, can we sing it again for Ms. Martin?"

The basic techniques of good singing are taught (pardon the cliché, not caught). Music teachers agree and would eagerly share this message with celebrities who try to sing "The Star-Spangled Banner" as they strive for high notes beyond their vocal capability, forget the words, or invent a new version altogether. Renée Fleming set a new standard when she sang "The Star-Spangled Banner" at Super Bowl 2014. One news report said 78 percent of listeners that day called her performance outstanding. She was the first opera singer invited to sing before a Super Bowl game. World Series 2014 was not lacking in star-spangled magnificence when Joyce DiDonato sang it a cappella. Around the world in 2014, Anna Netrebko sang the "Olympic Anthem" before the games at Sochi. Longtime soccer fan Placido Domingo performed with soprano Ana Maria Martinez and pianist Lang Lang in concert two days before the finale of the World Cup in Rio de Janeiro. Someone cleverly named this phenomenon Arias in the Arena.

Teaching *against* bad singing rarely succeeds. If children and adults are self-conscious about singing, they may wither under even well-meaning criticism. Teaching *about* differing styles of singing is more appropriate and effective. The latter approach opens up all sorts of music-learning possibilities; in particular, it allows teachers to push past "I don't like that" to initiate creative discoveries of why and how singers and singing are often distinctively different. Learning that people of all cultures sing together in families and communities informs children of the significance of singing from ancestral song lines to the living present.

Choosing songs that make children want to sing begins with songs you love to hear. Many songs for children require rehearsal time beyond the limits of the classroom schedule. If time and opportunity allow, conducting a children's chorus brings enriched musical rewards for students and teachers. Whatever your musical preferences, be mindful that children's musical tastes are more eclectic than is generally known, especially for songs composed or arranged by master composers and set to poetic texts. The following recommendations range from simple to moderate in complexity, from exquisite melodies to whimsical texts, and all beautifully written for children's voices:

"Velvet Shoes" (unison), Randall Thompson; "Simple Gifts" (SA), "I Bought Me a Cat" (SA), "At the River" (SSA), Aaron Copland; *Two Stevenson Songs:* "Rain" (unison) and "Where Go the Boats" (unison), Carlisle Floyd; "Before the Paling of the Stars" (unison), John Boda, music, and Christina Georgina Rossetti, words; "Finnegin's Fugue" (SA), Frederick Silver; "Hymn to Freedom" (unison), Oscar Peterson; "The Carol of the Birds" (SA), John Jacob Niles; *A Child's Book of Beasts, Set 1:* "The Hippopotamus,"

"The Rhinoceros," "The Frog" (SA), Jean Berger, music, and Hilaire Belloc, words; "Horace Was a Hippo" (unison), Arthur Boynon, music, and Irene Glass, words; "If I Were" and "The Moon" (unison), Elizabeth Palmer; "Ladybird" (Katalinka) (SSA), Zoltán Kodály; *Three Children's Songs:* "The Singers" (unison), R. Vaughn Williams; "Early One Morning" (unison/descant), traditional English song arranged by Geoffrey Shaw; "The Path to the Moon" (unison), Eric Thiman; "Oft in the Stilly Night," traditional Irish song (unison/descant), words by Thomas Moore, arranged by Eric Thiman; "May Day Carol" (SA), arranged by Deems Taylor; "How Far to Bethlehem?" Mary E. Caldwell, music, words adapted from G. K. Chesterton by Mary E. Caldwell; "Sheep May Safely Graze" (unison), J. S. Bach; "Alleluja" (SSA), W. A. Mozart.

UNWELCOME INCIDENTS IN THE CLASSROOM

A word about the problem of solving problems. We need new words for classroom control, behavior management, and discipline problems. No wonder when children learn they must be controlled, managed, and disciplined, they resist. "You're not the boss of me!" There was a kindergarten boy who announced his status as he entered the music room: "I am the CEO of this class!" A struggle of wills between teacher and child followed until one of us preferred to play the conga drum instead of giving orders.

Children like this little CEO struggle against authority at the first whiff of power. It is difficult for some students to accept the social mores and principles of conduct at school. When children have experienced extremes of rigid control or neglectful permissiveness, they have difficulty accepting rules of behavior and cannot fit comfortably in their classrooms. Many children suffer unmistakable challenges physically, emotionally, and socially. Some live without permanent homes or biological parents, and many come to school hungry and sleepy. All these conditions are obstacles to learning. Even children with warm beds and good food, who live with financially secure families, are known to suffer emotional and social neglect. Know that there is no comparison between these differing populations, rather these comments refer to distinctions between life experiences. Children learn what they are able to learn. How they act and react, ways they speak and listen demand our dedicated attention and understanding. Each child is extraordinary, whether impeded or assisted at home, in school, in the neighborhood, the community, and the larger society.

Knowing how to help students adjust to classroom rules and requirements is far more difficult than knowing how to teach music. Teachers in new positions frequently want to know how to reach disruptive students and students who refuse to participate. Going to a new school and facing the unknown gives children and teachers the jitters. New music teachers are often adrift and on their own professionally. Look at their challenges. Each teacher is a one-of-a-kind specialist in music. Some teach every child in their school, even those with populations of more than a thousand students. Music teachers meet their classes ranging for thirty to fifty minutes at a time over a five- to eight-day rotation. Given cuts in positions, some music teachers travel between two or more schools. In my experience, most purchase some or all of their own music-teaching materials. This work is truly difficult and truly magnificent. The good news is that after the first year, teachers have acquired personal knowledge of returning students and are familiar with the school faculty, staff, and community environment. No longer novices, they have learned successful strategies to use and not so successful ones to avoid. Experience will have raised new questions and led to further study and implementation.

Comparable to questions about new materials are questions about student behavior, how to discourage misbehavior, and reward appropriate behavior. Reward systems, specific to music and music making are in common use; but if the rewards invite competition among individuals, groups, or classes, or if rewards are delayed until the end of the week, month, or term, the results may be less effective. Rewards refer to remuneration, incentive, or a prize. In contrast, recognition is associated with acknowledgment and appreciation or a gesture of thanks. Young students respond favorably to recognition offered immediately for attentiveness, responsiveness, participation, and performance. "Well done" is often the best reward. Instead of food, toys, or anything expensive, the best acknowledgments are plentiful, all the same, and changed often, such as pirate gold coins, an Olympic medal lariat, a certificate, or similar tokens of appreciation.

Then, there are times when all else fails with a troubled student. You and your student need privacy (even in a corner of the classroom) to establish eye-to-eye contact, develop rapport, and initiate communication: "What's going on with you today? How can I help? "What do you need—some time to yourself?" "Something to do? Want to be my assistant? Help set up instruments? Distribute materials?"

When too many individuals are disruptive at the same time, the situation may require a surprising and immediate halt to the lesson. "We are unable to continue." If needed, collect materials, and invite students to be seated. Speak directly with honest sensitivity concerning disappointment with the present behavior, verbal disrespect, and bullying, and that such unruly behavior deprives everyone of making music. A follow-up or alternative approach invites students to participate in a group think tank: Ask students to form a circle and sit on the floor (or chairs). Announce guidelines for discussion: agreed-upon topics, one speaker at a time, and use of "I" statements. Comments ought to be recorded by students; and agreements posted for reference and review. But before things go wrong:

1. Establish clear, specific, and brief "Do's and Do Not Do's."
2. Lighten up. Use humor.
3. Be fair. Apologize when you are wrong.
4. Don't go crazy over every little thing.
5. Be consistent. If it's not okay, it's not okay all the time. If it's not okay for one, it's not okay for everyone, including the teacher.
6. Don't break your own rules. Students will catch you out.
7. Rig the environment with enthusiasm and joy of learning.
8. Pay attention to individuals. Be aware of the vibes of the whole class.
9. Set a lively pace.
10. Don't talk too much. Stop saying the same things over and over.
11. Teach music with music.
12. Listen to the children.

This is another technique that may work for you: Surprise and dazzle your students with big words, foreign language phrases, and how-would-Shakespeare-say-it? Make up your own exhortations and use foreign languages your students are not likely to understand.

> *Prithee, repose yourselves.*
> *You have lost your aplomb.*
> *You tread upon my patience.*
> *Give thy thoughts no tongue.*
> *Errare humanum est* (To err is human).
> *Acta est fabula* (The play is over).

One of the most wonderful, superior, excellent, and very good way to get students' attention and interrupt what or who needs interrupting: Invoke Star Power! "Someone today will be selected for a powerful musical position." Place a music stand facing the students; and with a baton, show and tell what the conductor does as you play a recording of music they know. Choose big, orchestral music: themes from any *Star Wars* movie, *Indiana Jones, Jaws*; Sousa marches and patriotic songs, "Semper Fidelis," "The Stars and Stripes Forever," "The *Washington Post* March," "The Marines' Hymn," Army, and Air Force and Navy Songs, "You're a Grand Old Flag." Students feel powerful when they conduct works like Beethoven's Symphony no. 5, movement 1, Mozart's *Eine kleine Nachtmusik*, Grieg's "In the Hall of the Mountain King," or Wagner's "Ride of the Valkyries." A few well-placed small percussion instruments throughout the group add a flair of authenticity and offer an opportunity for more and more students to participate as players.

MAKING MUSIC RULES THAT MATTER

There is no shortage of rules, principles of behavior, and guidelines established by local administrators or generated by teachers, but not all best apply in the music classroom. The music room is different from all other settings, including the contained classroom with desk and chairs for general studies and tests, the art room, and areas for physical education.

Each of the following statements may be displayed as a poster and presented to students. Not only did my students like the rules, they liked to quote them. Select one or more of these statements, or create your own, and in a timely manner, discuss expectations with students.

> Don't Make Me Use My Opera Voice
> Music Rocks! Music Teacher Rules!
> Get Your Brain in the Game
> Make Music, Not Noise
> Obey, You Play
> Do Not Obey, You Do Not Play
> R-E-S-P-E-C-T
> Be the Best You Can Be!

In 1990 the United Nations Convention on the Rights of the Child enacted forty-two articles on human rights and fundamental freedoms for the protection of children. All children under the sun, moon, and stars have the right to be protected and cared for, to be free from abuse and neglect, and to have a name and a country, a high standard of health care, free access to education for the development of each child's personality, talents, and abilities, physically and mentally, for respect and freedom in the spirit of peace, understanding, equality, and friendship. Children also have the right to rest and to play. Framed by the ideas presented here, it follows that teachers are not managers, disciplinarians, controllers, or guards. We serve children as facilitators of learning, leaders of exploration and invention, and mentors of achievement. We are makers of imagination and wizards of wonder.

> *Come take me out of this dull world,*
> *For I would ride with you upon the wind,*
> *Run on the top of the dishevelled tide,*
> *And dance upon the mountains like a flame.*
> —W. B. Yeats, *The Land of Heart's Desire*

NOTES

1. CDs and DVDs are used throughout this work. Depending on the technology available, many teachers use MP3 or other online resources, and digital devices.

2. YouTube may be restricted from access in your classroom, as it was mine. However, you may use this source for finding new material and planning.

3. Credit for this clever title goes to a six-year-old girl enrolled in a music class for children at Teacher's College-Columbia, directed by Lori Custodero. She shared this delightful anecdote.

4. Evaluation Guidelines:

1. Provide challenge levels appropriate to student's musical skills and understanding through opportunities for exploring and making music.

2. Conduct informal evaluation of musical skills, knowledge, and previous experiences with music.

3. Observe student's musical responses:

    a. Moving to beat, accents, rhythm patterns
    b. Playing instruments with rhythmic and tonal accuracy
    c. Listening to and identifying music's fundamental elements, characteristics, qualities, and styles
    d. Singing with accurate pitch and suitable range
    e. Creating and improvising music and musical ideas with instruments
    f. Evaluate student's skills, knowledge, and understanding, and provide immediate feedback with encouragement and correction, as needed.

4. Conduct formal evaluation of musical skills, knowledge, and understanding through assessment: Complete or Incomplete; Satisfactory or Unsatisfactory.

    a. Question and Answer
    b. Quiz and Examination
    c. Reports
    d. Projects, individual and/or small group
    e. Presentations, individual and/or small group
    f. Performances, individual and/or small groups

5. Behavioral Objectives:

    a. Increase focus on learning.
    b. Increase attention to instructions.
    c. Provide rules for music learning.
    d. Convey expectations for behaviors for specific music activities.

6. Music Classroom Rules

    a. Enter music room quietly.
    b. Stay in line order.
    c. Wait for person ahead to sit down.
    d. Be seated.
    e. Show readiness to make music.
    f. Listen to instruction.

7. More detailed directives

    g. "Make music, not noise with mouth, hands, feet, chairs" or any other object.
    h. "Start playing instruments on time, stop on time."
    i. "Take instrument given." "You get what you get—don't get upset."

    j. "Refuse, and you lose a turn to play."
    k. "When the music stops, you stop."
    l. "Follow instructions the first time given."

8. Consequences for refusal to follow rules

    a.   Warning
    b.   Sign music rulebook, tell what you did, explain what you should have done.
    c.   Time-out
    d.   Phone parent.
    e.   File incident report.

9. Recognition of Excellence

    a.   Sign music excellence book.
    b.   Choose special privilege from the options offered.

FIVE

Perspectives

Voices of Teachers

Education is not the piling on of learning information, data, facts, skills, or abilities—that's training or instruction—but is rather making visible what is hidden as a seed.
—Thomas Moore

Who you are contributes to why and what you teach as well as how. If you ask lifelong teachers why they teach, some say "to make a difference," or "for the love of children." Teachers would not say "for the money" or "summer vacations." There exists something inherently strong and even courageous in those who would be teachers, especially ones who never give up, give in, or give out.

Teaching has never been easy. Meet Elsie in *Very Lovingly Yours, Elsie: Adventures of an Arizona Schoolteacher, 1913–1916.* Similar to many well-educated young women of her time, Elsie hoped to share her love of learning by teaching, even if it meant moving to a remote area without the comforts of home, especially electricity and running water. Her story is vividly expressed in the journals, letters, and photographs she kept. In her day, teachers' personal lives were closely scrutinized. Elsie explained:

Teachers are not to keep company with men.
Women may not dye their hair.
Teachers may not loiter downtown in ice cream stores.
Dresses must be no more 2 inches above the ankle.
Teachers are not to dress in bright colors.

A generation later, Pat Duffy Hutcheon, in *Lonely Trail: The Life Journey of a Freethinker*, writes of her childhood in a rural Alberta, Canada, schoolroom and her life as a young schoolteacher. She emerged from poverty and neglect to become a master teacher, a brilliant scholar, and the author of more than eighty publications, including several textbooks. She became an international spokesperson and recipient of many awards for her humanitarianism. This is how Pat Hutcheon describes a special teacher from her childhood:

> Looking back from all my subsequent years of experience within the field of education, I give Miss Tewksbury credit for much of what I was able to do with my life. I was at a crucial stage of development, and she proved to be an inspiration to me in many ways. For instance, she worked hard to build up the sparse library contained within two tiny book shelves. One way she did this was to encourage us to contribute spare books from our homes. I was already an avid reader, but was embarrassed about the fact that we didn't seem to own much in the way of books. (p. 32)

The National Public Radio series *Options in Education* explored the topic "What Makes a Good Teacher Good?" In this episode, John Merrow, educational journalist and researcher, reported that good teachers have similar traits with other good teachers: (a) they are lifelong learners; (b) they have high expectations of their students; they encourage risk taking and accept errors; (c) they respect creative independence; (d) they have deep knowledge of what they teach; (e) they value humor; (f) they are flexible, insightful; and (g) they are compelling and convincing communicators.

Everyone knows a good teacher. When Diane Ravitch, best-selling author and research professor at New York University, asked, "Who was your favorite teacher?" many people who follow her blog responded. Ravitch summarized their comments:

> People write about teachers who were strict and demanding; they write about teachers who were passionate about their subject; they write about teachers who were inspiring; they write about teachers who were fun and pulled pranks; they write about their physics teacher, their German teacher, their music teacher. I couldn't find anyone who wrote about the teacher who raised their test scores.[1]

Here are a few entries edited for brevity and identity:

- To my high school German teacher, I attribute my lifelong interest in language and linguistics, which became my profession. From my high school band director, I gained some much-needed discipline and the importance of experiencing esprit de corps at a period where that made a huge positive difference.
- When he taught me eighth-grade history and English, he was a first-year teacher (about to be not invited back next year). I believe he took the job at [a junior high school] in Bay County, Florida,

because the school was being integrated. It was ugly, and he stood up to Klan members right in the school administration.

- Grade 6, PS 101. Brooklyn, NY. 1964. On Friday afternoons, she would turn off the lights around 2:30 and read poetry. On the day she read *The Tell-Tale Heart*, I was hooked forever on poetry and all types of literature. I do something similar in my class and my kids can't wait. [She] also returned all the Beatles magazines she confiscated during the year.
- [My] third grade teacher at [an elementary school] in Wilmette, Illinois. She was so nice, and every child in her class loved her. (So many decades later, I can recognize the power of simply being nice.)

Some bloggers wrote about being a teacher:

- The biggest compliment I have ever gotten was when a black child in an all-black special ed class I taught music to in Kansas City told his teacher that I was fair. I loved that. I worked hard for that. And actually, it's not so hard if you were treated fairly as a child, and I was. I hope you were, too.
- And this, from personal experience, came from one of my kindergarten students: "Hey Mom, see that big kid over there? She's my music teacher."

THE NEW NORMAL

There will always be teachers who merit their students' lasting appreciation and fondness. As there will always be teachers who do their best to meet all challenges and battle all obstacles for the good of the students they teach. While teachers share common characteristics, each one differs according to his or her life story, circumstances, personality, and talents. Efforts to standardize teacher behavior ignore the distinctive personalized foundation of teaching and learning.[2] "Teacher-proof" curriculum bolstered by technology stymies the very accountability targeted; and worse, it insults teachers and demoralizes the profession. Talk of "bad" teachers and "failing" schools[3] is ablaze on the tongues of self-appointed pundits,[4] corporate nabobs,[5] and state legislators[6] on the dole. With so many talking heads and billionaire experts, the general public only hears sound-bites about "bad" teachers and "failing" schools. Without authenticated information made widely accessible in the popular media, deceptive reports and unfounded opinions persist as "truth."[7] Push has come to shove back. Now is the time for teachers, parents, and all citizens who care about public education and the democracy that holds it together, to commit to a plan of action based on four principles:

Knowledge: *Get informed*

Speech: *Speak out loud*
Conviction: *Take a stand*
Contribution: *Make a difference*

TEACHING MUSIC UNDER NEW RULES

Where did the new rules come from? The National Governors Association and the Council of Chief State School Officers developed the Common Core State Standards with strong involvement by the U.S. Department of Education. The Common Core State Standards are based on the following precepts:

- Research and evidence based
- Clear, understandable, and consistent
- Aligned with college and career expectations
- Based on rigorous content and the application of knowledge through higher-order thinking skills
- Built upon the strengths and lessons of current state standards
- Informed by other top-performing countries to prepare all students for success in our global economy and society

    According to the best available evidence, the mastery of each standard is essential for success in college, career, and life in today's global economy. (www.corestandards.org)

At this writing, the arts standards are being field tested and made ready for implementation. Outlines and details for understanding and using the standards are presented at www.nationalartsstandards.org. "National Core Arts Standards are designed to guide the delivery of arts education in the classroom with new ways of thinking, learning, and creating. The standards also inform policy-makers about implementation of arts programs for the traditional and emerging models and structures of education." Examination of the new ways reveals a significant departure from the National Standards for Music in place since 1994. In fact, the differences are such that talking about music takes precedence over making music.[8] The new music standards emphasize conceptualization that is more relevant to language and mathematics than the ways of knowing music.[9]

The 1994 Content Standards (K–4 and 5–8) uphold that which makes music education musical:

1. Singing alone and with others, a varied repertoire of music.
2. Performing on instruments, alone or with others, a varied repertoire of music.
3. Improvising melodies, variations, and accompaniments.
4. Composing and arranging music within specific guidelines.
5. Reading and notating music.
6. Listening to, analyzing, and describing music.
7. Evaluating music and music performances.
8. Understanding relationships between music, the other arts, and disciplines outside the arts.
9. Understanding music in relation to history and culture.

Every course in music, including performance courses, should provide instruction in creating, performing, listening to, and analyzing music, in addition to focusing on its specific subject matter. (*National Standards for Arts Education*, 1994, p. 59) [10]

The 2014 Core Standards [11] (pre-K–8) emphasize knowing about music through cognitive processes, judging, reasoning, and evaluating:

1. Creating
   a. Imagine

Generate musical ideas for various purposes and contexts.
Enduring Understanding: The creative ideas, concepts, and feelings that influence musicians' work emerge from a variety of sources.
Essential Question: How do musicians generate creative ideas?

   b. Evaluate and Refine

Evaluate and refine selected musical ideas to create musical work(s) that meet appropriate criteria.
Enduring Understanding: Musicians evaluate, and refine their work through openness to new ideas, persistence, and the application of appropriate criteria.
Essential Question: How do musicians improve the quality of their work?

   c. Present

Share creative musical work that conveys intent, demonstrates craftsmanship, and exhibits originality.
Enduring Understanding: Musicians' presentation of creative work that conveys intent, demonstrates craftsmanship, and exhibits originality.
Essential Question: When is creative work ready to share?

2. Performing
   a. Select

Select varied musical works to present based on interest, knowledge, technical skills, and content.

Enduring Understanding: Performers' interest in and knowledge of musical works, understanding of their own technical skill, and the context for a performance influence the selection of repertoire.

Essential Question: How do performers select repertoire?

b. Analyze

Analyze the structure and context of varied musical works and their implications for performance.

Enduring Understanding: Analyzing creators' context and how they manipulate elements of music provides insight into their intent and informs performance.

Essential Question: How does understanding the structure and context of musical works inform performance?

c. Interpret

Develop personal interpretations that consider creators' intent.

Enduring Understanding: Performers make interpretive decisions based on their understanding of content and expressive intent.

Essential Question: How do performers interpret musical works?

d. Rehearse, Evaluate, and Refine

Elevate and refine personal and ensemble performances individually or in collaboration with others.

Enduring Understanding: To express their musical ideas, musicians analyze, evaluate, and refine their performances over time through openness to new ideas, persistence, and the application of appropriate criteria.

Essential Question: How do musicians improve the quality of their performances?

e. Present

Perform expressively, with appropriate interpretation and technical accuracy, and in a manner appropriate to the audience and context.

Enduring Understanding: Musicians judge performances based on criteria that vary across time, place, and cultures. The context and how a work is presented influence the audience response.

Essential Question: When is a performance judged ready to present? How do context and the manner in which musical work is presented influence audience response?

3. Responding
   a. Select

Choose music appropriate for a specific purpose or context.

Enduring Understanding: Individuals' selection of musical works is influenced by their interests, experiences, understandings, and purposes.

Essential Question: How do individuals choose to experience?

b. Analyze

Analyze how the structure and context of varied musical works inform the response.

Enduring Understanding: Response to music is informed by analyzing context (social, cultural, and historical) and how creators and performers manipulate the elements of music.

Essential Question: How does understanding the structure and context of music inform a response?

c. Interpret

Support interpretations of musical works that reflect creators'/performers' expressive intent.

Enduring Understanding: Through their use of elements and structures of music, creators, and performers provide clues to their expressive intent.

Essential Question: How do we discern the musical creators' and performers' expressive intent?

d. Evaluate

Support evaluations of musical works and performances based on analysis, interpretation, and established criteria.

Enduring Understanding: Through their use of elements and structures of music, creators, and performers provide clues to their expressive intent.

Essential Question: How do we discern the musical creators' and performers' expressive intent?

4. Connecting
    a. Connect

Synthesize and relate knowledge and personal experiences to make music.

Enduring Understanding: Musicians connect their personal interests, experiences, ideas, and knowledge to creating, performing, and responding.

Essential Question: How do musicians make meaningful connections to creating, performing, and responding?

b. Connect

Relate musical ideas and works with varied context to deepen understanding.

Enduring Understanding: Understanding connections to varied context and daily life enhances musicians' creating, performing, and
responding.

Essential Question: How do the other arts, other disciplines, contexts,
and daily life inform creating, performing, and responding to music?

TOWARD CONSTRUCTING CURRICULUM

Standards are not the curriculum. Standards are statements of what students should know and when they should know it. Furthermore, standards are not even standardized. States and local districts set standards
for levels of attainment according to specified goals pertaining to all subjects, for all students, and at the same time.[12] Curriculum—derived from
what students should know and when—is the manifestation of the discipline's inherent content. Instruction is the delivery system, the how-to
teaching strategies aimed to accomplish the goals of the curriculum.

For decades, elementary school music teachers have studied and applied systems of thought by Carl Orff, Zoltán Kodály, Émile Jacques-
Dalcroze, and Shinichi Suzuki. Leading music educators have developed
curricula and instructional methods according to each of these approaches. Teachers attend workshops and courses designed to promote
musicianship and pedagogy. These programs are successful because the
quality of the program is maintained and most offer certification for those
who qualify. Participants attend classes in person where they develop
strong ties of mutual support.

Additionally, there are many other sources for teaching music, particularly online. Yet, given so many choices, it can be frustrating for teachers
to decide which publications meet their needs for what to teach and how
to organize lessons and develop teaching strategies. In any case, when
teachers enter their classrooms, the work is all their own. Doug Goodkin,[13] internationally acclaimed music educator, posted this:

> Teach what you love. Teach what you know. Teach who you are. Don't
> follow someone else's plan. But know the territory of the Orff pedago-
> gy a la Levels I, II, III to narrow your choices for developmentally
> appropriate material. Then make a list of pieces, games, songs, activ-
> ities that are meaningful to you. Including things you did as a kid.
> That's your curriculum.

THE BIG PICTURE

Prevailing efforts to reform public education, insure teacher accountability, and improve student achievement have failed to produce the very
results predicted. A cohort of "reformers" who seek to privatize public

education claim that our schools are broken, teachers are inadequate, and students lack "grit" and determination. "Failing" neighborhood schools are closing and charter schools are moving in. There's talk that charter schools will attract new families, land values will go up, and condos and malls will follow. School business is big business.

Common Core's theoretical fragmentation defeats the true purposes of education. In what future world might students armed with less knowledge and fewer skills succeed in a competitive global economy?[14] Efforts to reconstruct public education by regulation from the market-place and dominance of technology are misplaced and shortsighted. By the time these realities are in place, the peopled-world will have evolved anew.[15]

Daniel H. Pink, in his introduction to *A Whole New Mind: Why Right-Brainers Will Rule the Future* (2006) wrote:

> The future belongs to a very different kind of person with a very different kind of mind—creators and empathizers, inventors, designers, storytellers, caregivers, consolers, big picture thinkers—will now reap society's richest rewards and share its greatest joys. (p. 1)
>
> We are moving from an economy and a society built on the logical, linear, computerlike capabilities of the Information Age to an economy and a society built on the inventive, empathic, big-picture capabilities of what's rising in its place, the Conceptual Age. (pp. 1–2)

EDUCATION FOR THE TWENTY-FIRST CENTURY

In spite of standardized testing, data gathering, and rule binding, let us not forget that we—teachers and students—are living spiritual beings in company of one another. Lest our educational perspectives become insular and our practices limited, we must look for a broad vision of knowing and living together in the world. *Everyone has the right to a quality education.* The United Nations Educational, Scientific, and Cultural Organization dedicates its resources to education throughout the world.[16] In the "Four Pillars of Learning," UNESCO expands the intentionality of learning:

- Learning to Know: to provide the cognitive tools required to better comprehend the world and its complexities, and to provide an appropriate and adequate foundation for future learning.
- Learning to Do: to provide the skills that would enable individuals to effectively participate in the global economy and society.
- Learning to Be: to provide self-analytical and social skills to enable individuals to develop to their fullest potential psychosocially, affectively as well as physically, for an all-round complete person.
- Learning to Live Together: to expose individuals to the values implicit within human rights, democratic principles, intercultural

understanding and respect and peace at all levels of society and human relationships to enable individuals and societies to live in peace and harmony (http://en.unesco.org/themes/education-21st-century).

POSTSCRIPT

Where is the wisdom we have lost in knowledge?
Where is the knowledge we have lost in information?
—Thomas Stearns Eliot, "Choruses" from *The Rock*

NOTES

1. Diane Ravitch's blog (dianeravitch.net), August 11, 2013.
2. Yet the "reforms" currently in operation magnify the personal difficulties facing students and their teachers. So far, music teachers are not required to administer standardized tests; however, they are under pressures that affect all teachers when student evaluations are linked to teacher accountability, performance, and evaluation. Standardized testing in music may or may not be actualized. Until such time, some districts are using students' test results in reading and math for music teacher evaluations.
3. Who decides if a good teacher is bad? "Bad" teachers and "failing" schools are like monsters under the bed—no one can see them, but the very idea scares many people silly.
4. "Media Matters conducted an analysis of education coverage on weeknight cable news programs so far in 2014 to determine how many of the show's guests who discussed the topic were educators. Across MSNBC, CNN, and Fox, only 9 percent of guests in education segments were educators. On segments in which there was a substantial discussion of domestic education policy between January 1, 2014, and October 31, 2014, there were 185 guests total on CNN, MSNBC, and Fox, only 16 of whom were educators, or 9 percent." November 20, 2015. Lis Power, Hilary Tone, and Jessica Torres, researchers.
5. Profits from charter schools are big business. Privatization of public education, closing public schools, and opening charter schools in the same community is highly profitable for investors and start-up corporations. "Charter School Vulnerabilities to Waste, Fraud, and Abuse," May 2014, a report from the Center for Popular Democracy and Integrity in Education exposed $100 million in taxpayer funds meant for children instead lost to fraud, waste, and abuse by charter schools in fifteen states. Given these findings, the authors have expanded their investigation state by state to determine the extent of charter school corruption. This is a summary of their findings: "The report draws upon news reports, criminal complaints and more to detail how, in just 15 of the 42 states that have charter schools, charter operators have used school funds illegally to buy personal luxuries for themselves, support their other businesses, and more. The report also includes recommendations for policymakers on how they can address the problem of rampant fraud, waste and abuse in the charter school industry. Both organizations recommend pausing charter expansion until these problems are addressed."
6. Follow the money: ALEC, the American Legislative Exchange Council, established in 1973, offers corporate America the opportunity to shape legislation that serves its profit-gaining interests in statehouses around the country. "To accomplish this control of the legislative process, ALEC provides forums (conferences that double as posh vacations for legislators and their families) in which both companies and

legislators meet in order to write and vote on 'model' legislation. The agreed-upon 'model' legislation is then advanced in statehouses nationwide, carried home with legislators like a corporate-financed virus, with ALEC providing abundant reminders and 'talking points' (a short list of statements that offer the appearance of having detailed knowledge of an issue) for legislators to help ensure passage of bills designed to fill those corporate-sponsor coffers" In addition to corporations and legislators, ALEC members include corporate trade groups, nonprofits, law and lobbying firms, and government groups.

7. Diane Ravitch, a research professor of education at New York University, is the most influential voice today speaking truth to powerful politicians and influential billionaires and their efforts to "reform" public education. Her latest book, *Reign of Error: The Hoax of the Privatization Movement and the Danger to America's Public Schools*, is a best seller. She blogs at dianeravitch.net; the site has had nearly 19 million page views in less than three years (April 2015). Interviews with Ravitch are found on Bill Moyers & Company; Jon Stewart; Tavis Smiley; Terry Gross, NPR; Christine Romans, CNN, *Inside the Academy*, a four-part series interview.

8. Veteran music teacher Kirk Kassner, "Some Concerns about the Core Standards," wrote, "The CSs [Common Core Standards] rely on the constructivist approach, asking even young children to give their opinions about music. While I believe there are useful places for a constructivist approach, I agree with Kodály that the children need to learn some basic musical vocabulary, listen to a great deal of music, and be involved in many musical activities before they have sufficient experience to construct their own ideas." —*Music Educators Journal*, December 2014.

9. The National Association for Music Education's (NAfME) support of the Common Core State Standards is disappointing but understandable. Powerful political pressure in the name of public education "reform" all but silenced voices of opposition (http://musiced.nafme.org/musicstandards/).

10. Why take time to ask children what they know, think, and feel about music? Some say, "I could teach a new song in the time it takes you to do that." While such observations might sound reasonable, the intent is still a distortion—analogous to an untrue pitch—of music's broader purpose. Whether by note or rote, learning without context limits children's expressive intelligence, just as skill and drill alone restricts children's understanding of music.

11. www.corestandards.org.

12. Repeating text from the preface, pp. ix–x. Secretary Duncan made enthusiastic predictions for success even while Common Core Standards were under construction and revision and before the corresponding assessments were designed. In a speech before the American Society of Newspaper Editors in June 2013, Duncan spoke of the benefits of Common Core: Teachers in different states could use the same lesson plans; a child in Mississippi would face the same expectations as a child in Massachusetts; and children of military personnel could move across the world "without a hitch" in their schooling. He added, "I believe the Common Core State Standards may prove to be the single greatest thing to happen to public education in America since *Brown v. Board of Education*."

13. Doug Goodkin is a highly respected and innovative music educator and author of many books based on the philosophy and music practices of Orff Schulwerk. He granted permission to include his comment about creating curriculum, a position fundamental to the premise of this book.

14. It is not surprising that language and mathematics are the keystones of the Common Core State Standards initiative, and that mastery of the requisite skills in these disciplines leads to "college, career, and life in today's global economy." Given the narrow focus on these high-stakes tested subjects, all other disciplines essential to children's education are left out. Importance dedicated to language and mathematics leaves very little time in the school day for music, art, social studies, science, and recess.

15. "Do not confine your children to your learning, for they were born in another time." — Hebrew Proverb (www.quotes.net/quote/40464). "Your children are not your own. They are the sons and daughters of Life's longing for itself." — Kahlil Gibran, *The Prophet*. New York: Alfred A. Knopf, 1923.

16. Joseph Steiglitz, Nobel Laureate and professor at New York's Columbia University, wrote:

> Children, it has long been recognized, are a special group. They do not choose their parents, let alone the broader conditions into which they are born. They do not have the same abilities as adults to protect or care for themselves. That is why the League of Nations approved the Geneva Declaration on the Rights of the Child in 1924, and why the international community adopted the Convention on the Rights of the Child in 1989.
>
> Sadly, the United States is not living up to its obligations. In fact, it has not even ratified the Convention on the Rights of the Child. The US, with its cherished image as a land of opportunity, should be an inspiring example of just and enlightened treatment of children. Instead, it is a beacon of failure—one that contributes to global sluggishness on children's rights in the international arena. (www.project-syndicate.org/)

Epilogue

On the Cusp of Possibility

Ultimately, it is my hope that this work will contribute to curriculum decisions and instructional choices, inspire creativity, and encourage individuality. Moreover, I wish to commend to you the children—all those who look to you for acceptance beyond instruction, playfulness over efficiency, and open-mindedness to see the world with a child's-eye view. When children's minds and hearts are young, they are eager to know and learn. They are joyful, compassionate, honest, trusting, and resilient. Their needs—to play, pretend, and explore, and to sing, dance, and make music—must be safeguarded. As their teachers, we are challenged to create pedagogy and possibilities that guarantee each child a meaningful education in music, embraced by enduring compassion and esteem.

> *So, if you hear me, tell me that you hear,*
> *Lest I grow weary and forget to sing . . .*
> —Robert Nathan[1]

NOTE

1. Quote from "The heart in wonder, like a lonely wren," in *Selected Poems of Robert Nathan*, "Sonnet VI." New York: Alfred A. Knopf, 1935.

Postscript

*I have gathered a posy of other men's [people's] flowers and nothing
but the thread that binds them is my own.*
—Michel de Montaigne

Bibliography

Aardema, Verna, and Beatriz Vidal. *Bringing the Rain to Kapiti Plain: A Nandi Tale*. New York: Dial, 1981.

Ackerman, Karen, and Stephen Gammell. *Song and Dance Man*. New York: Alfred A. Knopf, 1988.

Ada, Alma Flor. *Pío Peep! Traditional Spanish Nursery Rhymes*. New York: HarperCollins, 2003.

Anderson, Laurie Halse, and Matt Faulkner. *Thank You, Sarah: The Woman Who Saved Thanksgiving*. New York: Scholastic, 2002.

Anderson, M. T., and Petra Mathers. *Strange Mr. Satie*. New York: Viking Press, 2003.

Beethoven Lives Upstairs. Children's Group, 2002. CD.

Boynton, Sandra. *Dog Train*. Book and CD edition. New York: Workman Publishing, 2006.

Brien, Eileen, and Jane Chisholm. *The Usborne Internet-Linked Introduction to Music*. London, UK: Usborne, 2000.

Bryan, Ashley. *All Night, All Day: A Child's First Book of African-American Spirituals*. Selected and illustrated by Ashley Bryan; musical arrangements by David Manning Thomas. New York: Atheneum, 1991.

Bucchino, John, and Anna-Liisa Hakkarainen. *Grateful: A Song of Giving Thanks*. Book and CD edition. New York: HarperCollins, 2003.

Bunting, Eve, and Wendy Popp. *One Candle*. New York: Joanna Cotler, 2002.

Burleigh, Robert, and Leonard Jenkins. *Langston's Train Ride*. New York: Orchard, 2004.

Carle, Eric. *I See a Song*. New York: Thomas Y. Crowell, 1973.

Carter, Prudence L. *Closing the Opportunity Gap: What America Must Do to Give All Children an Even Chance*. New York: Oxford University Press, 2013.

Chalk, Gary. *Yankee Doodle: A Revolutionary Tail*. New York: Dorling Kindersley, 1993.

Children's Singing Games. Performers School Children. Saydisc Records, 1983. CD.

Coleman, Evelyn, and Aminah Brenda Lynn Robinson. *To Be a Drum*. Morton Grove, IL: Albert Whitman, 1998.

Copland and the American Sound. Performed by Michael Tilson Thomas and the San Francisco Symphony, 2006. DVD.

Crawford, Mel. *Gerald McBoing Boing: Based on the Academy Award-Winning Motion Picture*. New York: Random House, 2000.

Dillon, Leo, and Diane Dillon. *Rap a Tap: Here's Bojangles—Think of That*. Pine Plains, NY: Live Oak Media, 2005.

Dodds, Dayle Ann, and Rosanne Litzinger. *Sing, Sophie!* Cambridge, MA: Candlewick, 1997.

Edelman, Marian Wright, and Adrienne Yorinks. *Stand for Children*. New York: Hyperion for Children, 1998.

Feliciano, José, and David Diaz. *José Feliciano's Feliz Navidad*. New York: Scholastic, 2004.

Fitzgerald, Ella, and Van Alexander. *A-Tisket, A-Tasket*. New York: Philomel, 2003.

Fleming, Candace, and Giselle Potter. *Gabriella's Song*. New York: Atheneum for Young Readers, 1997.

Ford, Michael, and Sandra Boynton. *Rhinoceros Tap*. Book and CD edition. New York: Workman Publishing, 2004.

Fowke, Edith. *Canada's Story in Song*. Rev. ed. Toronto, Canada: Gage Publishing, 1965.

Fowke, Edith, and Alan Mills. *Singing Our History: Canada's Story in Song*. Toronto, Canada: Doubleday Canada, 1984.

Fox, Dan, and Claude Marks. *Go In and Out the Window: An Illustrated Songbook for Young People*. New York: Metropolitan Museum of Art, 1987.

Frazee, Marla. *Hush, Little Baby: A Folk Song with Pictures*. San Diego, CA: Browndeer, 1999.

Grigg, Carol. *The Singing Snow Bear*. Boston, MA: Houghton Mifflin, 1999.

Guthrie, Woody, and Vladimir Radunsky. *Bling Blang*. Cambridge, MA: Candlewick, 2000.

Hoberman, Mary Ann, and Nadine B. Westcott. *The Lady with the Alligator Purse*. Boston, MA: Joy Street, 1988.

Hoberman, Mary Ann, and Nadine B. Westcott. *There Once Was a Man Named Michael Finnegan*. New York: Little, Brown, 2001.

Hoberman, Mary Ann, and Nadine B. Westcott. *Miss Mary Mack*. New York: Little, Brown, 2004.

Hughes, Langston, and Matthew Wawiorka. *The Book of Rhythms*. New York: Oxford University Press, 1995.

Isadora, Rachel. *Bring On That Beat*. New York: Putnam, 2002.

Kindersley, Anabel, and Barnabas Kindersley. *Celebrations!* New York: DK Publishing, 1997.

Kirp, David L. *Kids First: Five Big Ideas for Transforming Children's Lives and America's Future*. New York: PublicAffairs, 2011.

Kolar, Bob. *Do You Want to Play? A Book about Being Friends*. New York: Dutton Children's Books, 1999.

Laan, Nancy, and George Booth. *Possum Come a-Knockin'*. New York: Knopf, 1990.

Langstaff, John. *A Revels Garland of Song: In Celebration of Spring, Summer & Autumn*. Watertown, MA: Revels, 2003.

Langstaff, John, and George Emlen. *The Revels Book of Chanteys and Sea Songs*. Watertown, MA: Revels, 2006.

Langstaff, John, and George Emlen. *Celebrate the Winter: Winter Solstice Celebrations for Schools & Communities*. Watertown, MA: Revels, 2001.

Langstaff, Nancy, John Langstaff, and Jan Pienkowski. *Sally Go Round the Moon: Revels Songs and Singing Games for Young Children*. Watertown, MA: Revels, 1986.

Lithgow, John, and C. F. Payne. *The Remarkable Farkle McBride*. New York: Simon & Schuster for Young Readers, 2000.

Locker, Thomas. *Water Dance*. San Diego, CA: Harcourt Brace, 1997.

Locker, Thomas. *Cloud Dance*. New York: Voyager, 2000.

Long, Melinda, and David Shannon. *How I Became a Pirate*. San Diego, CA: Harcourt, 2003.

Manders, John. *Señor Don Gato: A Traditional Song*. Cambridge, MA: Candlewick, 2003.

Martin, Bill, and Vladimir Radunsky. *The Maestro Plays*. New York: Henry Holt, 1994.

McCully, Emily Arnold. *The Orphan Singer*. New York: Arthur A. Levine, 2001.

McGovern, Ann, and Simms Taback. *Too Much Noise*. Boston: Houghton Mifflin, 1967.

Medearis, Angela Shelf, and Daniel Minter. *Seven Spools of Thread: A Kwanzaa Story*. Morton Grove, IL: Albert Whitman, 2000.

Most, Bernard. *Cock-a-Doodle-Moo!* San Diego, CA: Harcourt Brace, 1996.

Neill, Mary Le Duc, and Leonard Weisgard. *Hailstones and Halibut Bones: Adventures in Color*. Garden City, NY: Doubleday, 1961.

Pellegrini, Anthony D. *The Future of Play Theory: A Multidisciplinary Inquiry into the Contributions of Brian Sutton-Smith*. Albany: State University of New York, 1995.

Polacco, Patricia. *John Philip Duck*. New York: Philomel, 2004.

Purton, Michael. *Show-Me-How I Can Make Music*. New York: Smithmark, 1996.

Raven, Margot Theis, and Earl B. Lewis. *Circle Unbroken: The Story of a Basket and Its People*. New York: Farrar, Straus & Giroux, 2004.

Ravitch, Diane. *The Death and Life of the Great American School System: How Testing and Choice Are Undermining Education*. New York: Basic Books, 2010.

Ravitch, Diane. *Reign of Error: The Hoax of the Privatization Movement and the Danger to America's Public Schools*. New York: Vintage, 2014.

Reimer, Bennett. *Seeking the Significance of Music Education: Essays and Reflections*. Lanham, MD: Rowman & Littlefield Education, 2009.

Reiser, Lynn. *Tortillas and Lullabies / Tortillas y Cancioncitas*. New York: HarperCollins, 1998.

Riggio, Anita. *A Moon in My Teacup*. Honesdale, PA: Caroline House / Boyds Mills Press, 1993.

Robinson, Sandra Chisholm, and Peter Grosshauser. *The Rainstick: A Fable*. Helena, MT: Falcon Press, 1994.

Roth, Susan L., and Angelo Mafucci. *Do Re Mi: If You Can Read Music, Thank Guido d'Arezzo*. Boston, MA: Houghton Mifflin, 2006.

Rudolph, Thomas E., and James Frankel. *YouTube in Music Education*. Milwaukee, WI: Hal Leonard, 2009.

Shange, Ntozake, and Romare Bearden. *I Live in Music: Poem*. New York: Welcome Enterprises, 1994.

Sweet, Melissa. *On Christmas Day in the Morning: A Traditional Carol*. Cambridge, MA: Candlewick, 1999.

Van Manen, Max. *Researching Lived Experience: Human Science for an Action Sensitive Pedagogy*. Albany: State University of New York, 1990.

Ward, Leila, and Nonny Hogrogian. *I Am Eyes: Ni Macho*. New York: Greenwillow Books, 1978.

Williams, Linda, and Megan Lloyd. *The Little Old Lady Who Was Not Afraid of Anything*. New York: HarperCollins, 1986.

Winter, Jonah, and Jeanette Winter. *Once upon a Time in Chicago: The Story of Benny Goodman*. New York: Hyperion for Children, 2000.

You Are My Little Bird. Performed by Elizabeth Mitchell. Smithsonian Folkways, 2006. CD.

Works Cited

Aaron Copland—Symphony No. 3, Billy the Kid (Suite). Performed by James Judd, New Zealand Symphony Orchestra. Naxos American Classics, 2000. CD.

All for Freedom. Performed by Sweet Honey in the Rock. Music for Little People, 1992. CD.

American Album, The. Performed by Leonard Slatkin, Saint Louis Symphony Orchestra. BMG Classics, 1991. CD.

Anderson, M. T., and Kevin Hawkes. *Handel: Who Knew What He Liked*. Cambridge, MA: Candlewick Press, 2013.

Bailey, Carolyn Sherwin, and Jacqueline Rogers. *The Little Rabbit Who Wanted Red Wings*. New York: Platt & Munk, 1988.

Barker, Roger G. *Ecological Psychology; Concepts and Methods for Studying the Environment of Human Behavior*. Stanford, CA: Stanford University Press, 1968.

Baylor, Byrd, and Tom Bahti. *When Clay Sings*. New York: Scribner, 1972.

Been in the Storm So Long: Spirituals, Folk Tales and Children's Games. Performed by Johns Island, South Carolina Singers. Smithsonian Folkways, 1990. CD.

Beethoven, Ludwig Van. *Beethoven's Wig 4: Dance Along Symphonies*. Cambridge, MA: Rounder Kids, 2009. CD.

Beethoven's Wig Sing Along Symphonies. Cambridge, MA: Rounder Kids, CD, 2002.

Bernstein, Leonard. *The Joy of Music*. New York: Simon & Schuster, 1959.

Bernstein, Leonard, and Isadore Seltzer. *Young People's Concerts*. New York: Simon & Schuster, 1970.

Bierhorst, John. *A Cry from the Earth: Music of the North American Indians*. New York: Four Winds Press, 1979.

Blacking, John. *How Musical Is Man?* Seattle: University of Washington Press, 1973.

Blow, Ye Winds in the Morning: Traditional Sea Songs, Dances and Chanteys. Performed by John Langstaff and others. Revels Records, 1992. CD.

Boynton, Sandra, and Michael Ford. *Blue Moo: 17 Jukebox Hits from Way Back Never: Deluxe Illustrated Songbook*. New York: Workman Publishing, 2007.

Brandt, Anthony, Molly Gebrian, and L. Robert Slevc. "Music and Early Language Acquisition." *Frontiers in Psychology*, 2012.

Britten, Benjamin, Anita Ganeri, and Ben Kingsley. *The Young Person's Guide to the Orchestra*. Book and CD. New York: Harcourt Brace, 1996.

Bronfenbrenner, Urie. *The Ecology of Human Development: Experiments by Nature and Design*. Cambridge, MA: Harvard University Press, 1979.

Bruner, Jerome S. *Toward a Theory of Instruction*. Cambridge, MA: Belknap Press, 1966.

Bühler, Charlotte Malachowski. *From Birth to Maturity: An Outline of the Psychological Development of the Child*. London: K. Paul, Trench & Trubner, 1935.

Bühler, Karl, and O. A. Oeser. *The Mental Development of the Child: A Summary of Modern Psychological Theory*. London: K. Paul, Trench & Trubner, 1930.

Caduto, Michael J., and Joseph Bruchac. *Keepers of the Animals: Native American Stories and Wildlife Activities for Children and Teacher's Guide*. Washington, DC: ERIC, 1991.

Callois, Roger. *Man, Play and Games*. Translated by Meyer Barash. Chicago: University of Chicago Press, 1961.

Campbell, Joseph, and Bill D. Moyers. *The Power of Myth*. New York: Doubleday, 1988.

Carey, Mariah. *Hero* (https://youtu.be/0IA3ZvCkRkQ).

Carpenter, Mary Chapin. *Halley Came to Jackson* (https://youtu.be/Om3j8VP1oCI).

Carpenter, Mary Chapin, and Dan Andreasen. *Halley Came to Jackson*. New York: HarperCollins, 1998. CD.

Castle, Caroline. *For Every Child: The Rights of the Child in Words and Pictures*. London: Red Fox Books, 2002.

Celenza, Anna Harwell, and JoAnn E. Kitchel. *Pictures at an Exhibition*. Watertown, MA: Charlesbridge, 2003.

Celenza, Anna Harwell, and JoAnn E. Kitchel. *The Heroic Symphony*. Watertown, MA: Charlesbridge, 2004.

Celenza, Anna Harwell, and JoAnn E. Kitchel. *Bach's Goldberg Variations*. Watertown, MA: Charlesbridge, 2005.

Celenza, Anna Harwell, and JoAnn E. Kitchel. *Gershwin's Rhapsody in Blue*. Watertown, MA: Charlesbridge, 2006.

Cobb, Edith. *The Ecology of Imagination in Childhood*. New York: Columbia University Press, 1977.

Cohlene, Terri, and Charles Reasoner. *Dancing Drum: A Cherokee Legend*. Mahwah, NJ: Watermill Press, 1990.

Cohlene, Terri, and Charles Reasoner. *Quillworker: A Cheyenne Legend*. Mahwah, NJ: Watermill Press, 1990.

Cohlene, Terri, and Charles Reasoner. *Turquoise Boy: A Navaho Legend*. Mahwah, NJ: Watermill Press, 1990.

Cole, Henry, and Marijka Kostiw. *Unspoken: A Story from the Underground Railroad*. New York: Scholastic, 2012.

Copland, Aaron. *What to Listen For in Music*. New York: McGraw-Hill, 1957. First published 1939.

Cowboy Album, The. Performed by Sons of the Pioneers, Roy Rogers, Marty Robbins, and others. Kid Rhino, 1992. CD.

Craft, Mahlon F., and Kinuko Craft. *Sleeping Beauty*. New York: Sea Star Books, 2002.

Crain, William. *Reclaiming Childhood: Letting Children Be Children in Our Achievement-Oriented Society*. New York: Henry Holt, 2003.

Curtis, Edward S., and Florence Curtis Graybill. *Edward Sheriff Curtis: Visions of a Vanishing Race*. New York: American Legacy Press, 1981.

Custodero, Lori, Claudia Cali, and Adriana Diaz-Donoso. "Tunes and Rhythms as Transitional Objects: Children's Spontaneous Musical Behaviors in the Subway." Proceedings for the International Society for Music Education, Brasilia, Brazil, 2014.

"Dance, Music, Theatre, Visual Arts: What Every Young American Should Know and Be Able to Do in the Arts: National Standards for Arts Education." Music Educators National Conference, Reston, Virginia, 1994.

Delpit, Lisa D. *Other People's Children: Cultural Conflict in the Classroom*. New York: New Press, 1995.

DePaola, Tomie. *The Legend of the Bluebonnet*. New York: G. P. Putnam, 1983.

Dewey, John. *Art as Experience*. New York: Minton, Balch & Company, 1934.

Dierickx, Mary B. *The Architecture of Literacy: The Carnegie Libraries of New York City*. New York: Cooper Union for the Advancement of Science and Art; New York City Department of General Services, 1996.

Dissanayake, Ellen. "Antecedents of the Temporal Arts in Early Mother-Infant Interaction." In *The Origins of Music*, 389–410. Edited by Nils. L. Wallin, Bjorn Merker, and Steven Brow. Cambridge, MA: MIT Press, 2000.

Eagle Walking Turtle. *Keepers of the Fire: Journey to the Tree of Life Based on Black Elk's Vision*. Santa Fe, NM: Bear, 1987.

Eisner, Elliot W. *The Arts and the Creation of Mind*. New Haven: Yale University Press, 2002.

Eliot, T. S. *The Complete Poems and Plays, 1909–1950*. San Diego, CA: Harcourt Brace Jovanovich, 1971.

Fantasia 2000. Performed by James Levine. Walt Disney Home Video, 2000. DVD.

Fassbender, Christopher. "Infants' Auditory Sensitivity towards Acoustic Parameters of Speech and Music." In *Musical Beginnings: Origins and Development of Musical*

Competence. Edited by Irene Dèliège and John A. Sloboda. New York: Oxford University Press, 1996.

Fernald, Anne. *Acoustic Determinants of Infant Preference for "Motherese."* Eugene, OR: University of Oregon, 1982.

Fiesta. Performed by Gustavo Dudamel, Simon Bolivar Youth Orchestra of Venezuela. Deutsche Grammophon, 2008. CD.

Folk Songs from Africa: Miriam Makeba, The Click Song. A World of Music, 1994. CD.

Fonteyn, Margot, and Trina Schart Hyman. *Swan Lake.* San Diego: Harcourt Brace Jovanovich, 1989.

Garbarino, J. "An Ecological Perspective on the Role of Play in Child Development." In *The Ecological Context of Children's Play,* 16–33. Edited by M. Block and A. Pellegrini. Norwood, NJ: Ablex, 1989.

Gatti, Anne, and Peter Malone. *The Magic Flute.* San Francisco: Chronicle Books, 1997.

God Bless America: The Ultimate Patriotic Album. Performed by London Festival Chorus and Orchestra, and others. Decca, 2002. DVD.

Goodall, Jane, and Phillip L. Berman. *Reason for Hope: A Spiritual Journey.* New York: Warner Books, 1999.

Goodlad, John I. *A Place Called School.* New York: McGraw-Hill, 2002.

Goodlad, John I. *Romances with Schools: A Life of Education.* New York: McGraw-Hill, 2004.

Great American Spirituals, vol. 9. Performed by Kathleen Battle, Barbara Hendricks, and Florence Quivar. Angel Records, 1992. CD.

Hodges, Donald. "Implications of Music and Brain Research." *Music Educators Journal: Special Focus Issue, Music and the Brain* 87, no. 2 (2002): 17–22.

Holmes, Edward. *The Life of Mozart.* London: J. M. Dent, 1932.

Hopkinson, Deborah. *Sweet Clara and the Freedom Quilt.* New York: Alfred A. Knopf, 1993.

Huizinga, Johan. *Homo Ludens: The Study of the Play-Element in Human Culture.* London: Routledge & Kegan Paul, 1955.

Hutcheon, Pat Duffy. *Lonely Trail: The Life Journey of a Freethinker.* Ottawa, Canada: Aurora Humanist Books, 2009.

Johanson, Donald, and Maitland Edey. *Lucy: The Beginning of Humankind.* New York: Simon & Schuster, 1981.

Johnson, Steven. *Where Good Ideas Come From: The Natural History of Innovation.* New York: Riverhead, 2010.

Jones, Theodore. *Carnegie Libraries across America: A Public Legacy.* Washington, DC: Preservation Press, 1997.

Journey of Dreams. Performed by Ladysmith Black Mambazo. Warner Bros., 1988. CD.

Langer, Susanne K. *Feeling and Form: A Theory of Art.* New York: Scribner, 1953.

Langer, Susanne K. *Philosophy in a New Key: A Study in the Symbolism of Reason, Rite, and Art.* 3rd ed. Cambridge, MA: Harvard University Press, 1957. First published 1942.

Lark in the Morn and Other Folksongs and Ballads, The. Performed by John Langstaff. Revels Records, 2004. CD.

Last Night of the Proms. Performed by Andrew Davies and the BBC Orchestra and Chorus. BBC Worldwide, 2001. DVD.

Levine, Ellen, and Kadir Nelson. *Henry's Freedom Box: A True Story of the Underground Railroad.* New York: Scholastic, 2007.

Lewin, K. "Environmental Forces." In *A Handbook of Child Psychology,* vol. 2, 590–625. New York: Russell & Russell, 1933.

Lithgow, John, and Boris Kulikov. *Carnival of the Animals.* New York: Simon & Schuster Books for Young Readers, 2004.

Littleton, Danette. "Child's Play: Pathways to Music Learning." *Promising Practices: Prekindergarten Music Education,* Music Educators National Conference, Reston, Virginia, 1988.

Littleton, Danette. "Influence of Play Settings on Preschool Children's Music and Play Behaviors." PhD diss. University of Texas at Austin, 1991.

Littleton, Danette. "Ecological Influences on Children's Musical Play." In *Music Education: Sharing Musics of the World*, 53–58. Twentieth World Conference of the International Society for Music Education, Seoul, Korea, 1992.

Littleton, Danette. "Cross-Cultural Perspectives on Preschool Children's Spontaneous Music Behaviors." In *Vital Connections: Young Children, Adults, and Music*. Columbia, MO: International Society of Music Education, 1994.

Littleton, Danette. "Cross-Cultural Perspectives on Young Children's Music-Making in the Context of Play." Proceedings of the Third Triennial European Society for Cognitive Sciences of Music, Uppsala, Sweden, European Society for Cognitive Sciences of Music, 1997.

Littleton, Danette. "Mother-Infant Play: The Cradle of Musicality." Respecting the Child in Early Childhood Music Education, Proceedings of the Eighth International Seminar of the Early Childhood Commission of the International Society of Music Education, Stellenbosch, South Africa, 1998.

Littleton, Danette. "Music Learning and Child's Play." *General Music Today* 12, no. 1 (1998).

Littleton, Danette. "Music in the Time of Toddlers." *Zero to Three* 23, no. 1 (2002): 35–40.

Manson, Christopher, and Marc Cheshire. *The Tree in the Wood: An Old Nursery Song*. New York: North-South Books, 1993.

Melmed, Laura Krauss, Ed Young, and Lee Lothrop. *The First Song Ever Sung*. New York: Lothrop, Lee & Shepard Books, 1993.

Mister Rogers' Songbook. Milwaukee, WI: Hal Leonard, 2015.

Montagu, Ashley. *Growing Young*. New York: McGraw-Hill, 1981.

Moorhead, Gladys Evelyn, and Donald Pond. *Music of Young Children*. Santa Barbara, CA: Pillsbury Foundation for Advancement of Music Education, 1978. [Book I. *Chant* (1941); Book II. *General Observations* (1942); Book III. *Musical Notations* (1944); Book IV. *Free Use of Instruments for Musical Growth* (1951).]

Morgan, Elaine. *The Descent of Woman*. New York: Stein & Day, 1972.

Morris, Desmond. *The Human Zoo*. New York: McGraw-Hill, 1969.

Mozart on Tour: London; Mantua. Performed by André Previn, Vladimir Askenazy, and Heidrun Holtmann. Brilliant Classics–Foreign Media Group, the Netherlands, 2014. DVD.

Mozart, Wolfgang Amadeus, and Hans Mersmann. *Letters of Wolfgang Amadeus Mozart*. New York: Dover, 1972.

My Favorite Heroines: World's Greatest Opera Stars. Performed by Mirella Freni, "Un bel di," and others. Decca, 1994. CD.

Nathan, Robert. *Selected Poems of Robert Nathan*. New York: Alfred A. Knopf, 1935.

Nation at Risk, A: The Imperative for Educational Reform. Washington, DC: National Commission on Excellence in Education, 1983.

New Orleans Playground. Putumayo Kids, 2006. CD.

Nouwen, Henri J. M. *Reaching Out: The Three Movements of the Spiritual Life*. Garden City, NY: Doubleday, 1975.

Nutcracker, The. Performed by the New York City Ballet. Warner Bros., 1997. DVD.

Oakley, Kenneth Page. *Man the Tool-Maker*. Chicago: University of Chicago Press, 1957.

Ode to Freedom: The Celebration Concert from Berlin. Performed by Leonard Bernstein and Selected Members of Worldwide Orchestras and Choruses. EuroArts, Germany, 1989. DVD.

Olatunji: Drums of Passion. Performed by Babatunde Olatunji. Sony, 2002. CD.

Paley, Vivian Gussin. *White Teacher*. Cambridge, MA: Harvard University Press, 1979.

Paley, Vivian Gussin. *Bad Guys Don't Have Birthdays: Fantasy Play at Four*. Chicago: University of Chicago Press, 1988.

Paley, Vivian Gussin. *You Can't Say You Can't Play*. Cambridge, MA: Harvard University Press, 1992.

Paley, Vivian Gussin. *Kwanzaa and Me—A Teacher's Story.* Cambridge, MA: Harvard University Press, 1995.

Paley, Vivian Gussin. *The Kindness of Children.* Cambridge, MA: Harvard University Press, 1999.

Paley, Vivian Gussin. *A Child's Work: The Importance of Fantasy Play.* Chicago: University of Chicago Press, 2004.

Papouček, Hanus. "Musicality in Infancy Research: Biological and Cultural Origins of Early Musicality." In *Musical Beginnings: Origins and Development of Musical Competence,* 37–55. New York: Oxford University Press, 1996.

Papouček, Mechthild. "Melodies in Caregivers' Speech: A Species Specific Guidance Towards Language." *Early Development and Parenting* (1994): 5–17.

Parten, Mildred. "Social Participation among Pre-School Children." *Journal of Abnormal and Social Psychology* 27 (1932): 243–269.

Parten, Mildred. "Social Play among Preschool Children." *Journal of Abnormal and Social Psychology,* 28 (1933): 136–147.

Paynter, John, and Peter Aston. *Sound and Silence: Classroom Projects in Creative Music.* London: Cambridge University Press, 1970.

Paynter, John, and Janet Mills. *Thinking and Making: Selections from the Writings of John Paynter on Music in Education.* Oxford: Oxford University Press, 2008.

Pellegrini, Anthony D. *The Oxford Handbook of the Development of Play.* New York: Oxford University Press, 2011.

Perlmutter, Richard, and Maria Rosetti. *Beethoven's Wig.* Cambridge, MA: Rounder Books, 2005.

Piaget, Jean. "Marxists Internet Archive." Marxists Internet Archive. January 1, 1962. Accessed January 25, 2015.

Piaget, Jean. *Play, Dreams and Imitation in Childhood.* New York: Norton, 1962.

Pictures at an Exhibition. Performed by Vladimir Askenazy and the Philharmonia Orchestra of London. Decca, 1990. CD.

Pink, Daniel H. *A Whole New Mind: Why Right-Brainers Will Rule the Future.* New York: Riverhead, 2006.

Pitts, Stephanie. *Chances and Choices: Exploring the Impact of Music Education.* New York: Oxford University Press, 2012.

Polanyi, Michael. *Personal Knowledge: Towards a Post-Critical Philosophy.* Chicago: University of Chicago Press, 1958.

Pond, Donald. "The Young Child's Playful World of Sound." *Music Educators Journal* (1980): 38.

Power of Myth, The. Performed by Joseph Campbell and Bill Moyers. 2000. DVD.

Prokofiev, Sergey, and Maria Carlson. *Peter and the Wolf.* New York: Viking Press, 1982.

Rachlin, Ann, and Susan Hellard. *Famous Children: Bach.* Hauppauge, NY: Barrow's, 1992.

Rachlin, Ann, and Susan Hellard. *Famous Children: Brahms.* Hauppauge, NY: Barrow's, 1992.

Rachlin, Ann, and Susan Hellard. *Famous Children: Mozart.* Hauppauge, NY: Barrow's, 1992.

Rachlin, Ann, and Susan Hellard. *Famous Children: Schubert.* Hauppauge, NY: Barrow's, 1992.

Rachlin, Ann, and Susan Hellard. *Famous Children: Tchaikovsky.* Hauppauge, NY: Barrow's, 1992.

Read, Herbert. *Education through Art.* New York: Pantheon, 1958.

Reimer, Bennett. *A Philosophy of Music Education.* Englewood Cliffs, NJ: Prentice Hall, 1970.

Roberts, Elsie Reed Hayes, and Barbara Anne Waite. *Very Lovingly Yours, Elsie: Adventures of an Arizona Schoolteacher, 1913–1916.* Vista, CA: Palomar Mountain Bookworks, 2011.

Rubinstein, Arthur. *My Young Years.* New York: Alfred A. Knopf, 1973.

Schiller, Friedrich. *On the Aesthetic Education of Man in a Series of Letters.* Boston: Little, Brown, 1845.

Seuss, Dr. *The Lorax.* New York: Random House, 1971.

Sing Along with Putumayo. Putumayo Kids, 2004. CD.

Singer, Dorothy G., and Jerome L. Singer. *The House of Make-Believe: Children's Play and the Developing Imagination.* Cambridge, MA: Harvard University Press, 1990.

Smilansky, Sara. *The Effects of Sociodramatic Play on Disadvantaged Preschool Children.* New York: Wiley, 1968.

Songs for Singing Children. Performed by John Langstaff. Revels Records, 1996. CD.

Songs from the Neighborhood: The Music of Mister Rogers. Performed by Amy Grant, John Pizzarelli, Toni Rose, and others. Family Communications, 2005. CD.

Spencer, Herbert. *The Principles of Psychology.* New York: D. Appleton, 1897.

Stern, Daniel N. *The Interpersonal World of the Infant: A View from Psychoanalysis and Developmental Psychology.* New York: Basic Books, 1985.

Strauss, Valerie. "Test-Weary Second-Grader Asks School Board: 'Is That All That Matters to Grown-Ups?'" www.washingtonpost.com/blogs/answer-sheet/wp/2015/01/17/test-weary-second-grader-schools-state-school-board-is-that-all-that-matters-to-grown-ups/.

Sutton-Smith, Brian. *The Ambiguity of Play.* Cambridge, MA: Harvard University Press, 1997.

Swan Lake. Performed by American Ballet Theatre. Educational Broadcasting Corporation, 2005. DVD.

Trehub, Sandra. "The Perceptions of Musical Patterns by Human Infants: The Provision of Similar Patterns by Their Parents." In *Comparative Perceptions: Basic Mechanisma,* vol. 1, 429–459. New York: Wiley, 1990.

Trevarthen, Colwyn. "Musicality and the Intrinsic Motive Pulse: Evidence from Human Psychobiology and Infant Communication." In *Musicae Scientiae,* Special Issue, 1999/2000.

Trevarthen, Colwyn, and Stephen Malloch. *Communicative Musicality: Exploring the Basis of Human Companionship.* Oxford: Oxford University Press, 2009.

Ustinov, Peter. *Dear Me.* Boston: Little, Brown, 1977.

Ustinov, Peter. *Quotable Ustinov.* Thorndike, ME: G. K. Hall, 1998.

Venezia, Mike. *George Gershwin.* Chicago: Children's Press, 1994.

Venezia, Mike. *Wolfgang Amadeus Mozart.* Chicago: Children's Press, 1995.

Venezia, Mike. *Getting to Know the World's Greatest Composers: George Handel.* New York: Children's Press, 1998.

Venezia, Mike. *Getting to Know the World's Greatest Composers: Johann Sebastian Bach.* New York: Children's Press, 1998.

Venezia, Mike. *Getting to Know the World's Greatest Composers: Johannes Brahms.* New York: Children's Press, 1998.

Venezia, Mike. *Getting to Know the World's Greatest Composers: Ludwig Van Beethoven.* New York: Children's Press, 1998.

Venezia, Mike. *Getting to Know the World's Greatest Composers: Peter Tchaikovsky.* New York: Children's Press, 1998.

Vygotsky, Lev. *Thought and Language.* Translated by Dr. Anne Parsons. Revised and edited by E. Hanfmann and G. Vaklar.

Wadsworth, Olive A., and Anna Vojtech. *Over in the Meadow: A Counting Rhyme.* New York: North-South Books, 2002.

We Are America's Children. Performed by Ella Jenkins. Smithsonian Folkways, 1989. CD.

Weeks, Marcus. *Mozart: The Boy Who Changed the World with His Music.* Washington, DC: National Geographic, 2007.

Welty, Eudora. *One Writer's Beginnings.* Cambridge, MA: Harvard University Press, 1999. First published 1984.

Whitehead, Alfred North. *Science and the Modern World.* Cambridge, MA: Cambridge University Press, 1926.

Whitehead, Alfred North. *The Aims of Education and Other Essays*. New York: Macmillan, 1929.

Whiting, Jim. *The Life and Times of Leonard Bernstein*. Hockessin, DE: Mitchell Lane, 2005.

Wild Mountain Thyme, The. Performed by John Langstaff and others. Revels Records, 1993. CD.

Willard, Nancy, and Leo Dillon. *The Sorcerer's Apprentice*. New York: Blue Sky Press, 1993.

Winter, Jeanette. *Follow the Drinking Gourd*. New York: Alfred A. Knopf, 1998.

Winter, Jonah, and Barry Blitt. *The 39 Apartments of Ludwig van Beethoven*. New York: Schwartz & Wade, 2006.

Wolfgang Amadeus Mozart: The Magic Flute. Performed by James Levine and the Metropolitan Opera, Orchestra, Chorus, and Ballet. Metropolitan Opera HD Live, 2006. DVD.

World Playground. Performed by various artists. Putumayo Kids, 1999. CD.

Yeats, W. B. *The Collected Poems of W. B. Yeats*. New York: Macmillan, 1956.

Young People's Concerts. Performed by Leonard Bernstein and the New York Philharmonic. Kultur International, 1990. DVD.

Zwerger, Lisbeth, and Pytor I. Tchaikovsky. *Swan Lake*. New York: North-South Books, 2002.

Index

Abbado, Claudio, 4
absolute pitch, 30
accountability, of teachers, xiii, xvin2, 122, 124n2
administrators, music teachers and, 104
adult intervention, 32
aesthetics, of play, 35
affective attunement, 40
Africa, 78, 78–81, 95
Afro-Cuban music, 95
The Aims of Education and Other Essays (Whitehead), 67–68, 68, 85
ALEC. *See* American Legislative Exchange Council
Alexander, Lamar, xi
The Ambiguity of Play (Sutton-Smith), 34
American Indians, 20–21, 96–99
American Legislative Exchange Council (ALEC), 124n6
American Recovery and Restoration Act, xii
analysis, 120, 121
animation, 12–13
Animusic, 7–8
Art as Experience (Dewey), 85
The Arts and the Creation of Mind (Eisner), 85
assessments, 98–99, 104–105, 113n4
authenticity, 90, 93
autodidactic, untaught learning, xix

Bach, Johann Sebastian, 22n5
ballet, 11
banjo, 81
Barker, Roger, 70
behavior: childhood, 63; environment and, 75; of infants, musical, 41; of mothers, musical, 41; music-play,

50–51; traits of children, xv, 70; unwelcome incidents in classroom, 109–111
Bernstein, Jamie, 2
Bernstein, Leonard, 2, 3–4, 5–6, 85, 86, 95; conducting of, 4–5; love of music, 2; on teaching, 2, 4; teaching methods of, 3; Watts and, 4, 22n9
Berry, Chuck, 81
big picture, 122–123
Billy the Kid, 8–11
biology, infants and, 63
Blacking, John, 39
Blue Moo, 91–92
blues, 81
Boynton, Sandra, 90–91
brain development, 40
Brandt, Anthony, 40
Bronfenbrenner, Urie, 70
Brown v. Board of Education, xii
Bruner, Jerome, 85, 87
Bühler, Charlotte, 33
Bühler, Karl, 33
Bush, George H. W., xi
Bush, George W., xi
Bush, Jeb, xi, xiv–xv

Callois, Roger, 34
Campbell, Joseph, 61, 69
Carey, Mariah, 66
Carlton, Larry, 23n18
Carnegie, Andrew, 1, 22n1
Carnegie Library, 1, 22n2
Carpenter, Mary Chapin, 62
"Cathedral Pictures," 8
CCSS. *See* Common Core State Standards
Center for Popular Democracy and Integrity in Education, 124n5